The Work
of Leaders

The Work of Leaders

How Vision, Alignment, and Execution Will Change the Way You Lead

Julie Straw
Mark Scullard
Susie Kukkonen
Barry Davis

WILEY

Cover design by Wiley
Copyright © 2013 by John Wiley & Sons, Inc. All rights reserved.

Published by Wiley
One Montgomery Street, Suite 1200, San Francisco, CA 94104-4594
www.wiley.com

No part of this publication may be reproduced, stored in a retrieval system, or transmitted in any form or by any means, electronic, mechanical, photocopying, recording, scanning, or otherwise, except as permitted under Section 107 or 108 of the 1976 United States Copyright Act, without either the prior written permission of the publisher, or authorization through payment of the appropriate per-copy fee to the Copyright Clearance Center, Inc., 222 Rosewood Drive, Danvers, MA 01923, 978-750-8400, fax 978-646-8600, or on the Web at www.copyright.com. Requests to the publisher for permission should be addressed to the Permissions Department, John Wiley & Sons, Inc., 111 River Street, Hoboken, NJ 07030, 201-748-6011, fax 201-748-6008, or online at www.wiley.com/go/permissions.

Limit of Liability/Disclaimer of Warranty: While the publisher and author have used their best efforts in preparing this book, they make no representations or warranties with respect to the accuracy or completeness of the contents of this book and specifically disclaim any implied warranties of merchantability or fitness for a particular purpose. No warranty may be created or extended by sales representatives or written sales materials. The advice and strategies contained herein may not be suitable for your situation. You should consult with a professional where appropriate. Neither the publisher nor author shall be liable for any loss of profit or any other commercial damages, including but not limited to special, incidental, consequential, or other damages. Readers should be aware that Internet Web sites offered as citations and/or sources for further information may have changed or disappeared between the time this was written and when it is read.

Wiley books and products are available through most bookstores. To contact Wiley directly call our Customer Care Department within the U.S. at 800-956-7739, outside the U.S. at 317-572-3986, or fax 317-572-4002.

Wiley publishes in a variety of print and electronic formats and by print-on-demand. Some material included with standard print versions of this book may not be included in e-books or in print-on-demand. If this book refers to media such as a CD or DVD that is not included in the version you purchased, you may download this material at http://booksupport.wiley.com. For more information about Wiley products, visit www.wiley.com.

Library of Congress Cataloging-in-Publication Data
CIP data is available on file at the Library of Congress.
ISBN 978-1-118-63657-2 (cloth)

Printed in the United States of America

FIRST EDITION

HB Printing   10 9 8 7 6 5 4 3 2 1

To the 1,800 members of the Inscape Network who give so generously of your time and talents to us and to your clients. Your partnership adds immeasurable value and helps make our work more meaningful.

Contents

Acknowledgments ix
Foreword by Leilani M. Poland xiii
Introduction xvii

1 Welcome to the Work of Leaders 1

VISION 11

2 Introduction to Crafting a Vision 13
3 Crafting a Vision Through Exploration 23
4 Crafting a Vision Through Boldness 33
5 Crafting a Vision Through Testing Assumptions 43
6 Summary of Crafting a Vision 53

ALIGNMENT 59

7	Introduction to Building Alignment	61
8	Building Alignment Through Clarity	69
9	Building Alignment Through Dialogue	79
10	Building Alignment Through Inspiration	89
11	Summary of Building Alignment	99

EXECUTION 105

12	Introduction to Championing Execution	107
13	Championing Execution Through Momentum	113
14	Championing Execution Through Structure	125
15	Championing Execution Through Feedback	135
16	Summary of Championing Execution	147

Afterword: Using VAE in Your Organization	153
Appendix A: The Development of the Work of Leaders VAE Model	161
Appendix B: Feedback Outtakes	189
References	193
Resources	197
About Inscape Publishing	201
About the Authors	203
Index	207

Acknowledgments

First and foremost, this book exists because of our relationships with a vast network of outstanding professional trainers, coaches, and consultants—the best of the best in the field of training and development. They have been our mentors and teachers, as well as our customers and business partners. Several Inscape Distributors were particularly generous in reviewing the manuscript for this book under tight timelines. In particular, Sue Hammond went above and beyond by providing us with astute developmental editing. We also want to thank Sue Bowlby, Jean Campana, Steve Dion, Chris Ewing, Sharon Ferraro, Joleen Goronkin, Murray Janewski, Sarah Kalicki-Nakamura, Lynne Kaplan, Janice Maffei, Jill McGillen, Leilani Poland, Cindy Sakai, Joanne Spigner, Rick Stamm, and Sal Silvester for taking the time to read the manuscript and provide helpful feedback. In addition, several of our Distributors shared client stories with us, including Carol Horner, Lisa Satawa, and Deb Terry. Finally, we are grateful to Keith Ayers, Anne Minton, Barb Stennes, and Roger Wenschlag for all the conversations that helped give context to this work.

We are also indebted to the clients of Distributors who used *Work of Leaders* and shared their experiences with us. Nathaniel Conn and Jeff Dahms were especially generous with their time, and their reflections on the VAE model helped bring our story to life. Indirectly, thousands of classroom learners supported our efforts by choosing to participate in our research after completing one of our assessments. Without them, we'd still be collecting data!

The authors are also lucky enough to work in an organization with talented individuals and high-functioning teams, and this project would not have been possible without everyone at Inscape Publishing. Special thanks to Rachel Broviak for facing the perils of putting our early ideas on paper, as well as for her flair with research and finding the right quotes. Jidana James helped us gather compelling stories and insightful feedback from many Inscape Distributors and their clients. Laurie Diethelm, Tracy LaChance, and Jeff Rauchbauer were willing to drop what they were doing to get the pieces that we needed when we needed them. The Inscape IT team, especially Don Hudson and Brad Meyer, made it possible for us to collect and retrieve the invaluable research data we use throughout the book. And our fearless leader, Jeffrey Sugerman, encouraged us to take on this challenge.

Special thanks to John Capecci for lending his expertise in effective storytelling. His thoughtful influence is woven throughout the book. We also are indebted to Emma Wilhelm, who created early drafts of our Work of Leaders story. Her work reviewing and consolidating all of the literature laid the groundwork for this book. And thanks to Aaron Rosell, who tackled the task of sorting and analyzing tens of thousands of comments with courage and humor.

We also want to thank our friends and colleagues at Wiley, especially Lisa Shannon and Cedric Crocker, whose efforts brought Inscape into the Wiley fold and allowed us to benefit from the resources of this well-respected, high-quality publisher. Matt Davis, our editor, has helped us navigate the path from concept to completion, and his flexibility and optimism have been much appreciated.

Finally, each of the authors would like to acknowledge other people in our lives who have made this project possible.

Julie would like to thank Jim Straw for his unwavering love and his support for her career ambitions, and Krystl, Kim, and Andy, for always understanding the balance of career and family. She also recognizes that, without the support of her Inscape team, especially Clare McInerney Stephenson, she would not have been able to pursue her passion for this book project.

Mark would like to thank his loving wife and feisty best friend, both of whom are Jill Scullard. His parents Julie and Mike Scullard also deserve an award for ensuring that he survived his adolescence. Thank you, guys. Finally, he needs to thank his daughter Eowyn, whose smile brings him joy and awe each and every morning.

Susie would like to thank Jukka Kukkonen for his love, encouragement, and good humor, and especially for getting up at 4:30 in the morning to help her draft a particularly difficult paragraph. She also owes a debt of gratitude to Barry

Davis and Ruth Walbon for lunchtime runs that helped to keep her on an even keel. Finally, thanks to Sonja and Henri for reminding her to laugh.

Barry would like to thank Shari Davis for being his true companion and showing him love every day. He thanks Carly, Noah, and Sydney for signing up to be his kids. And finally, he thanks all of his colleagues at Inscape and his friends and teachers in the Inscape Network. Without you, this work that he loves would not be possible.

Foreword

"Why should we listen to you.... what could you possibly teach us about leadership?" asked the former General turned bank executive. So began my first leadership challenge.

Did I have the vision to create a leadership program for the bank that would gain the approval and inspire the alignment of the entire executive team? And, if so, would the execution of that vision (my training program), create "better leaders"? Reflecting back on that early career challenge, I realize I was already using the principles inherent in the Work of Leaders model. Vision, Alignment and Execution are principals that transcend the test of time. And YES, my program was successful.

Today, I am President and Owner of TRC-The Resource Connection, a diversified and women-owned consulting and training firm. Since 1986, our mission has been to INSPIRE SUCCESS in the workplace. We connect our clients to learning resources, programs, and tools that improve the bottom line performance of their people. Through the use of assessment technology we help employees to develop sustainable skills that encourage responsible action.

For the past 26 years, I have worked closely with the Inscape team as an authorized distributor for their learning assessments and programs, perhaps most notably their signature DiSC® model. Over the last decade, I have partnered specifically with the authors of this book to successfully bring their insightful and validated assessment profiles and programs into Fortune 100-500 companies globally. These assessments are all uniquely designed to invite self-awareness and improve workplace performance at all levels within the organization. *Work of Leaders* is no exception.

While the authors of this book "lived" the work of leaders in their own organization, I often found myself experiencing that journey with them. Barry and Mark became champions of what could be—their Vision for new assessments and programs to accelerate the development of individual contributors, managers, and leaders in the workplace is unparalleled. Julie became the voice of the new Vision, helping me to Align the work I do with my clients so that I could better deliver extraordinary service during a time of transition. Susie used Execution to help Inscape through their own period of change with the most accurate, valid, and accessible tools to develop people and improve performance in the marketplace. As a team they were unstoppable!

Warren Bennis said it well, *"The most dangerous leadership myth is that leaders are born—that there is a genetic factor to leadership. That's nonsense; in fact, the opposite is* true. **Leaders are made** rather than born." If making leaders is important to you and your organization, the VAE model outlined in this book can guide you to that new reality. *The Work of Leaders* will enhance your strongest leaders, it will inspire your high potential leaders and it will provide a framework for success to those just beginning their leadership journey. I encourage you to put *The Work of Leaders* to the test within your organization.

Leilani M. Poland
President
TRC-The Resource Connection
www.resourceconnection.com

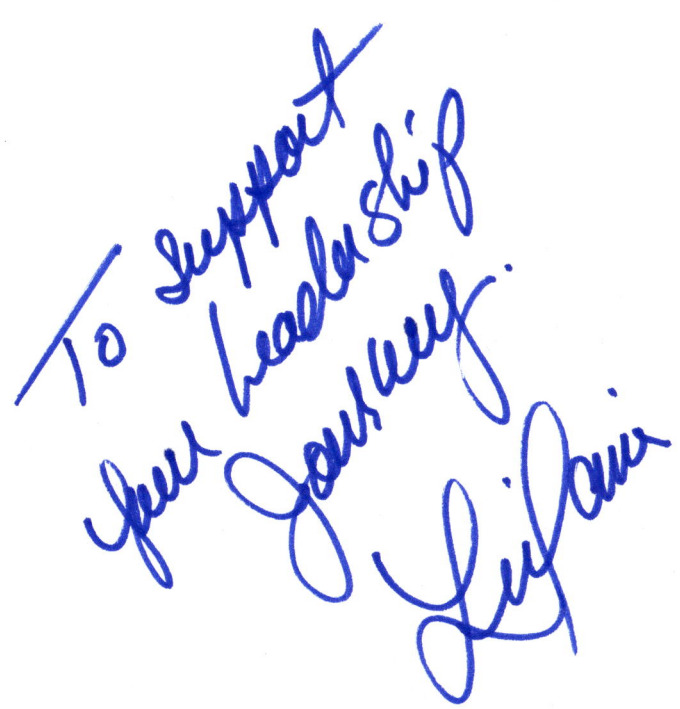

Introduction

Learning to be a leader is like learning to be a great athlete, musician, or artist. It's a capability that develops over time, through trial and error, hard work, and practice. Leadership is learned by doing, not simply by taking notes in a classroom.
Stanford Graduate School of Business

Consider these two scenarios.

Scenario One: The CEO sends out an email announcing the company's ambitious new sales goals and then takes the afternoon off to go golfing. The employees are left with no clear process, no strategy, and no delegation of responsibilities. Without direction or rationale, everyone is worried about making mistakes. There are whisper-sessions along the rows of cubicles. When something goes wrong, the finger-pointing begins. Trust and morale are low—and this is reflected not only in their ability to execute, but also in interactions with their customers.

Scenario Two: At the quarterly all-company meeting, the CEO stands before a simple map of the company's strategy. "These are the three platforms that lead to our success," he says. "If your work isn't related to or supporting one of these things, then please stop what you're doing—because you're not working on the right stuff." Since clearly establishing this vision, the company has been aligned—from the CFO who tracks the top line, to the customer-facing people who work on the front lines. All are focused on what they need to do to execute the vision and all are invested in the process. They openly collaborate, challenge one another, and celebrate accomplishments as they reach milestones.

We're guessing that if you've worked in business long enough, it's likely that there's something familiar to you in both of these scenarios. In our case, the four of us have worked together for the last ten years at Inscape Publishing, the company described in both scenarios. Of course we feel incredibly fortunate to be the company in Scenario Two today; to work in a stimulating and rewarding environment, to have built strong relationships with our colleagues, and to benefit from the rewards of excellent leadership. But like most companies, the fortunes of our company have waxed and waned more than once in our nearly forty-year history.

Inscape was founded in 1974, and by the end of the 1980s we were firmly established as the pioneer of DiSC®-based corporate training and assessment solutions. We had built a global network of thousands of independent training and development consultants who used our assessments and related training programs. We grew rapidly through the 1990s, but by 2000 the company faced two challenges. First, it was becoming clear that our strategy for going to market, based on paper-based assessments, was outmoded and not sustainable. What our customers wanted and needed were more advanced assessments that harnessed the power of the internet. We were, in essence, resting on our laurels: building and selling variations of a successful product rather than partnering with our customers to understand how their businesses and processes worked and could be adapted to a changing world.

Second, the leadership style adopted by Inscape's senior executives was also outmoded. Leadership was "caretaking" rather than proactive, both at the level of business strategy and in how we worked together. The effects could be felt throughout the company.

Executives held the strategy and vision close to their vests, so employees had little sense of direction, investment, or motivation. Individuals and business areas were in silos, which created uncoordinated efforts, not to mention internal competition for resources and rewards. We were a "meeting culture," with sluggish processes and unclear responsibilities. It wasn't pleasant or productive.

After the dot-com bubble burst in 2001, the company's ownership knew it was in trouble and named Jeffrey Sugerman as the new CEO. Jeffrey launched the transformation of Inscape from the first scenario we described to the second. He led the effort to help us define a new vision for our company, one that embraced the changes in the marketplace and placed our valued customers (our Distributors) at the center of our efforts. Jeffrey brought a style of leadership to Inscape that demanded a clearly communicated vision that all could understand and own; ground rules and expectations of how we would conduct ourselves, both internally and with our customers and vendors; and a positive work environment built upon openness, collaboration, and rigor. The transformation was not always comfortable or easy, but its effect was felt throughout the company as the culture changed gradually from one of mistrust to trust, from silos to collaboration, from fatigue to execution.

In short, Inscape made its way back to relevance in the marketplace through an almost textbook example of exemplary leadership. Together, we have seen first-hand how crafting a vision, building alignment around that vision, and championing the execution of that vision can transform a culture and save a company. We have also seen how essential these principles are not only to our CEO, but to the work of every leader at Inscape.

In 2007 we began our own in-depth study of what leaders at other companies do to help their organizations succeed. And after more than five years of research and development, we had boiled that work down to the same three things Jeffrey brought to Inscape—a passion and commitment to crafting a vision, building alignment, and championing execution.

In 2011, we began offering a leadership development program we call the Work of Leaders to help leaders at all levels, in all kinds of organizations, apply the simple concepts of vision, alignment, and execution (VAE) to their work. The program is available through our network of independent trainers and consultants, and the feedback we have received from them and their clients about the program has been overwhelmingly positive. The Work of Leaders is quickly becoming one of the most successful programs in the history of our company. With this book, our goal is to take the classroom experience that has been so valuable for thousands of leaders and introduce the VAE model to an even broader audience.

We are pleased to introduce *The Work of Leaders* to you and wish you success wherever you and your organization may be in your own leadership journey.

Julie Straw
Mark Scullard, Ph.D.
Susie Kukkonen
Barry Davis

1

Welcome to the Work of Leaders

Leadership is the capacity to translate vision into reality.
—Warren Bennis

Across from our Minneapolis office is a restaurant called The Super Moon Buffet. The word "super," however, is an almost coquettish understatement. *It is massive.* The theme is technically Chinese, but the ambition here goes way beyond what any single country could dream up. They've got sushi, French fries, ham, fresh fruit, roast duck, dim sum, apple pie, barbecued spare ribs, stir-fried frog legs, baby octopus, pork chitterlings. It's overwhelming. Each person has to come to terms with the Super Moon in his or her own way. Some people avoid paralysis by simply diving into the first dish that strikes them. Some rely on advanced mapping software. When we take out-of-towners there for lunch, they walk out the door and ask, "What just happened?"

This experience is not completely unlike sorting through the selection of leadership books on Amazon. *It is massive*, but not necessarily in a bad way. Just like the buffet, of course, there's some junk in there. (What is a chitterling anyway?) But mostly there are really brilliant, helpful, and practical insights. People who've spent a lifetime leading or studying leadership are willing to share their wisdom with the rest of us. The problem, however, is organizing and making sense out of all this information. To say the least, it's overwhelming.

We work for a company that's in the learning business. It's our job to make sure that people not only have access to information, but that they can actually absorb it. So we had a major task ahead of us when we set out to develop our own leadership training program about six years ago—make this wealth of leadership insight accessible to all kinds of people in all kinds of organizations. The key word here is "accessible."

Now, we know that people *want* to access this information, and we're not just talking about the people at the top. We asked more than 5,900 training participants in which skill areas they would voluntarily spend their time attending training. Table 1.1 shows the top five results.

Not surprisingly, people are most willing to attend training that has direct, concrete applications in their world—"technical knowledge related to my job." It's good to know how to do your job. But look at what's a close second with 81 percent: "Leadership skills." In fact, when we asked people what training would greatly increase their effectiveness

Table 1.1. Interest by Type of Training Program

Skill	Percent Who Would Attend the Training
Technical knowledge related to my job	86
Leadership skills	81
Innovative thinking skills	76
Management skills	76
Dealing with conflict or difficult people	74

at work, the number one answer, by far, was also leadership skills. More than half of the workers in our sample said they've read one or more leadership books in the past two years. Managers are more interested in attending leadership training than management training. People feel that there's a lot to learn—and there is.

But again, this information has to be *accessible* if it's going to make a real difference in anyone's work. So that's what we set out to do—make leadership accessible. In essence, our goal was to study all of the most respected thinking and research on leadership, focusing on common themes and major breakthroughs, and follow up with our own research, gaining clarification on the most promising ideas.

The first stage, our literature review, was, frankly, exhausting. Over the course of about five years, we worked with a team of people finding the best thinking on leadership. Now, it turns out that finding the best thinking also means reading a lot of the less-than-best thinking. But that's okay; nobody got hurt.

We also realized that if we wanted to come up with a truly comprehensive view of leadership, we would have to include writers from a broad range of perspectives:

Contemporary authors like Marcus Buckingham and Seth Godin	and	Classic authors like Peter Drucker and Warren Bennis
Authors who come from an academic background like Peter Senge and Daniel Goleman	and	Authors who come from a consulting background like Liz Wiseman and Patrick Lencioni
Leaders who have thrived in the non-profit sector like Frances Hesselbein and Gloria Duffy	and	Leaders who have thrived in the corporate world like Larry Bossidy and Harry Jensen Kraemer, Jr.
Authors who come from a highly philosophical perspective like John Maxwell and Max De Pree	and	Authors who come from a highly research-based perspective like Jim Collins and Jim Kouzes and Barry Posner

The goal was to pull out a simple structure that still captured the richness within all of this thinking. That is, what are the biggest, most important ideas?

Then we moved on to verify and build on what we had learned. We wanted clarification on these big, important ideas. How do they hold up under scrutiny? How do they apply to the work leaders do on a daily basis? As it turns out, we were in a highly enviable position to take on this sort of inquiry. We work for an organization that, among other things, helps hundreds of thousands of managers and leaders every year understand the relationship between their personalities and their work. We have as many as 3,500 people *a day* completing one of our online assessments, many of whom are gracious enough to help us out with our leadership research.

As a result, we can study the attitudes and behaviors of literally thousands of leaders every week. Collecting data of this magnitude usually takes months. Extensive resources are needed. Undergraduate psychology majors can be locked in rooms for weeks until they tabulate piles of surveys. Our setup, on the other hand, gave us the opportunity to quickly test hypotheses, look at the results, then test some more. We could pit grand theories and conventional wisdom against the real work that leaders do, every day. Ultimately, the VAE model in this book was created in ten stages of development, as shown in Table 1.2. You can read in more depth about this process and our research in Appendix A. And so we're happy to say that, throughout this book, we are able to provide you with the results from dozens of studies that we have conducted over the past five years with hundreds of thousands of participants. Given all of this information, however, we were sure not to lose sight of our end goal—to create a framework of leadership that was accessible and actionable for *everyone*—not just the CEOs or the Ph.D.s. We wanted to take the mystery out of leadership and spell out a leader's responsibilities as clearly as possible. The result was a leadership model of Vision, Alignment, and Execution—what we call the VAE model.

The VAE Model

In our view, leaders have three fundamental responsibilities: They craft a *vision,* they build *alignment,* and they champion *execution*. Of course, there's a lot of skill that

Table 1.2. Development of the VAE Model

	Stage	Description
FOUNDATION	1	*Leadership Literature Review:* We studied the works of 55 recognized thought leaders in the leadership field and identified major themes and patterns.
	2	*Personality Based Leadership Research:* We collected data to understand the influence of personality on leadership.
	3	*Analysis of 360-Degree Leadership Data:* We analyzed data from 360 raters to find the most important contributions and costly mistakes of leaders.
	4	*Survey of Training Industry:* In nine different studies, we surveyed learners in the training industry about their training experiences.
DEVELOPMENT	5	*Leadership Model Prototypes:* We created prototypes of the VAE model that provided a framework to test for both accuracy and resonance.
	6	*Subject-Matter Expert (SME) Reviews:* We approached hundreds of consultants, coaches, and corporate trainers for feedback on the model.
	7	*Classroom Testing:* We evaluated the experiences of thousands of learners who went through classroom training using the VAE model.
REFINEMENT	8	*Quantitative and Qualitative Feedback:* We augmented the research with online surveys and in-depth interviews of classroom facilitators.
	9	*Literature Review Update:* We revisited a wider range of social science research to understand leadership challenges from a broader perspective.
	10	*Supplemental Research:* We conducted dozens of studies to understand the VAE model on an applied, more granular level.

goes into each of these responsibilities. That, in fact, is what the rest of this book is about.

But, if you're the kind of person who absolutely insists on knowing what you're getting yourself into, here are some quick definitions.

- **Crafting a Vision:** imagining an improved future state that the group will make a reality through its work
- **Building Alignment:** getting to the point where everyone in the group understands and is committed to the direction
- **Championing Execution:** ensuring that the conditions are present for the imagined future to be turned into a reality

All three are part of a dynamic, fluid process. While there is a loose order implied in the VAE model, the actual Work of Leaders is not strictly sequential. Although it makes sense to craft a vision before aligning around it and executing on it, leaders are continually revisiting and reshaping their visions of the future. Likewise, we need to have buy-in before any major push toward execution, but maintaining alignment is an ongoing process.

There is, obviously, a great deal of complexity in doing the work of a leader, but the true value of this model is that it lays out a manageable, realistic framework to guide the process. The goal is to provide straightforward explanations of where you might choose to target your personal development efforts.

How This Book Is Organized

Accessibility is our overriding vision for this book. Therefore, the outline is pretty straightforward. Each of the three sections (Vision, Alignment, and Execution) has its own introduction followed by three drivers and a summary. A "driver" is a foundational element that lays the groundwork for each step of the process and makes it achievable. Within each of the drivers, you'll find two best practices, or specific behaviors that support the driver. So, for instance, the three drivers of Crafting a Vision are Exploration, Boldness, and Testing Assumptions. The two best practices of Exploration are Remaining Open and Prioritizing the Big Picture. Figure 1.1 shows the grand map.

You'll probably find that some of these drivers are second-nature to you. You'll have a hard time believing that someone could lead any other way. But as we see in every VAE training session, there are also some drivers that may be much more difficult. Everybody has at least a few areas where their initial reaction is, "You know what? That's just not my thing. What's the next one?" Ironically, those are the chapters that may help you the most. And that's why we've included "strategies for development" for each driver.

You certainly don't need to be a master in all of these areas, but our research suggests that, to be an effective leader, some level of skill in all drivers is a must. In the end, leadership development, like any personal development, is about energy. *Where* do you put your energy and *how much* do you put in? This book is about *where* to put your energy. You decide *how much*.

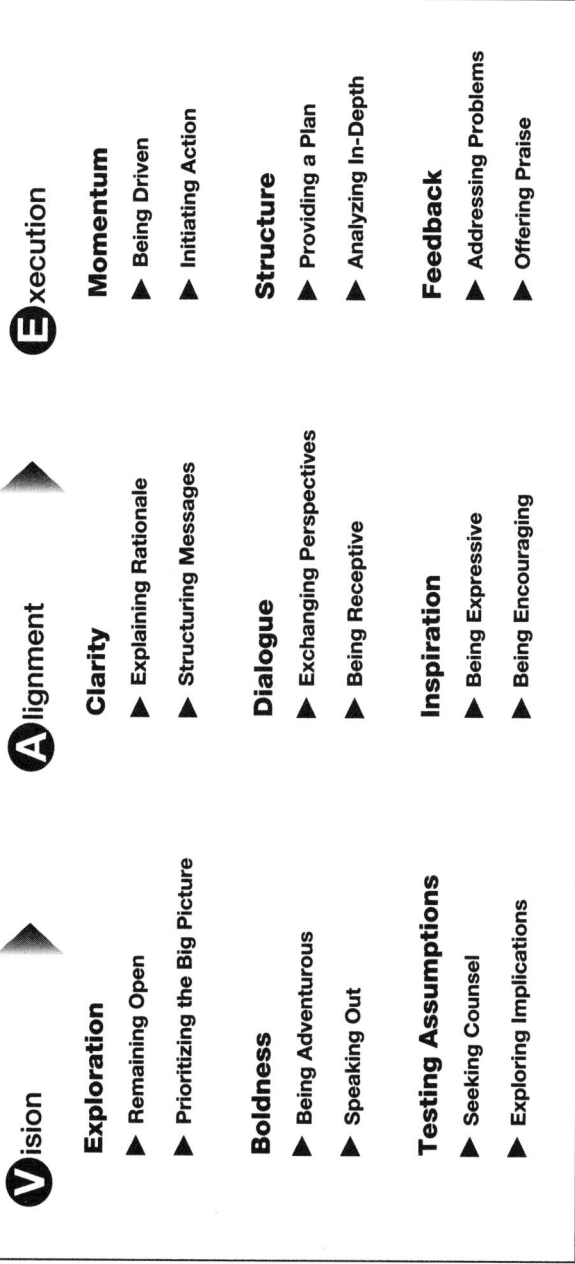

Figure 1.1. The Work of Leaders Overview

Cornerstone Principles of the Work of Leaders

- The VAE model approaches leadership as a one-to-many relationship, as opposed to the one-to-one relationship of management.
- The Work of Leaders is done by leaders at all levels. Whether you are a senior executive or a leader on the front line, the process of leadership follows the same path.
- The Work of Leaders is a collaborative process, but the journey to becoming an effective leader is a personal one. Some of the skills and best practices outlined here may come to you more easily than others.

PART 1

2

 **ision**
Exploration
Boldness
Testing Assumptions

**lignment**

**xecution**

Introduction to Crafting a Vision

The only thing worse than being blind is having sight but no vision.
—HELEN KELLER

In his book, *Stumbling on Happiness,* Harvard professor Daniel Gilbert makes a seemingly simple observation: The human being is the only animal that thinks about the future. When you come home from work and your dog has rearranged your living room, this was not part of some master plan. Maybe he was bored. Maybe he's mad at you. Maybe he was set up by the cat. But he definitely did not execute on a grand interior design vision. "The stuffing isn't quite working inside the couch. But what if we violently scattered it all over the carpet? It would really tie the room together." No dog has ever had this thought. So congratulations are in order. We are all automatically more qualified to lead than a black lab. We can envision a future that does not currently exist. It may not sound like much, but in biological terms, this is a truly astonishing ability.

The reason this skill probably doesn't strike you as terribly impressive is because you've been doing it for most of your life. When you sit down for an interview and the person across the desk asks you where you see yourself in five years, you're crafting a vision for your future. "I'll be starting my own company," "I'll be living abroad," "I'll be going back to graduate school." This isn't just your *plan* for the future. This is your *vision* of the future. You imagine what your world will look like in all sorts of interconnected dimensions—where you'll be living, the kind of salary you'll be pulling in, the relationships you'll have, the pants you'll be able to fit into, the respect you'll finally get at your high school reunion. It's a complete picture of how things will be. This is what leaders do when they craft a vision. They create a high-definition image of their world when all the work pays off.

What Exactly Do We Mean by Vision?

Now, if you ask anyone about vision, chances are you're going to hear Martin Luther King, Jr., and "I Have a Dream." In that speech, Dr. King didn't just describe the problems or list his goals. He painted a vivid picture of how our country could look if we set our minds to it. Southwest Airline's Herb Kelleher envisioned a work culture that was actually fun. Juliette Gordon Low imagined a world where girls could expand their roles in society, which led to the establishment of the Girl Scouts. Of course, then there's JFK's famous vision of putting a man on the moon before the end of the 1960s. And, oh yeah, don't forget Steve Jobs, Marie Curie, and Zeus. This is where we get ourselves in a bit of trouble. Vision, it might appear, is reserved for the elite, resplendent few.

What about the radiology supervisor at the regional hospital? The production manager at the cereal plant? The team leader at the Wash 'n Lube? When we limit the crafting of vision only to a chosen few at the top—the visionaries—and assume that only the grandest of visions counts, we get an insufficient view of how vision works. Every day, people in leadership roles at all levels and in all kinds of businesses craft visions of how things can be better. They call into question what we call "The Myth of the Mountaintop."

Rooted in an outmoded view of leadership that reveres visionaries, the myth goes something like this: a robed mystic sits high atop a mountain (or in the C-Suite), deep in contemplation until inspiration hits, and bam, the vision appears. The mystic descends into the village (or takes the podium at an all-company meeting), where eager followers flock to receive direction and instruction. Vision delivered, job done.

Sure, the characters are broadly painted—it's a myth, after all—but you begin to see where certain assumptions and misconceptions about vision and vision-crafting come from. The Myth of the Mountaintop assumes:

- The ability to craft a vision is innate, a trait possessed by only the truly gifted.

- Crafting a vision is an independent activity done by a lone genius.
- Crafting a vision is vaguely magical. It's ethereal and undefinable.
- A vision is something to be delivered from on high, mountaintop-down.

This mindset doesn't leave a whole lot of hope for most of us. We know where we graduated in our high school class and it wasn't anywhere near that snow-capped peak. Don't get us wrong, we have some expertise in our fields, people *seem* to respect us around the office, and we've even figured out how to use the automated paper towel dispenser in the bathroom—but no one has ever addressed us as *guru*, *sage*, or *the guiding light*.

So what if we create a fresh set of assumptions about vision, not just to make us feel better, but because we believe they actually do a better job at reflecting leadership in the real world? Consider that:

- Most people can learn how to craft an effective, compelling vision.
- Most great visions involve contributions from a wide range of people.
- The art of crafting a vision can be understood and practiced.
- Leaders at all levels are responsible for crafting a vision.

These are our assumptions for vision within our VAE model. This model is decidedly not about creating visionaries. It's about developing your leadership skills so you can pilot the vision-crafting process. If you're hoping to increase your effectiveness as a leader, this is good news, because the VAE model places crafting a vision within your reach. Regardless of how much or how little you have in common with Herb Kelleher, Juliette Gordon Low, or the ruler of Mount Olympus, you *will* be able to use the VAE model to lead the process of crafting a vision.

Okay, but why all this emphasis on vision in the first place?

The Importance of Crafting a Vision

What's the biggest single difference between experienced and inexperienced leaders? That was one of the big questions that we asked ourselves as we sifted through data from dozens of studies we've performed involving tens of thousands of leaders. To be sure, there were a lot of striking differences, which we'll share throughout this book, but one continually rose to the top. In the simplest possible terms, here it is: *Experienced leaders see vision as critical to a leader's work.* Among the novice leaders, some did recognize the importance of vision. On the other hand, many of them were quick to dismiss it. There was a lot of variation. Not with the experienced leaders, though. In this group we found significant consensus—crafting a vision for the group's future is paramount. In fact, this was one of the areas in which these leaders had the most agreement.

Now, we want to be clear here. Experienced leaders didn't say that vision was just critical to *their* work, as director or VP or CEO or maharajah. They said vision was critical to *every* leader's work. And this isn't just an academic observation. For years, we've had the privilege of working with hundreds of consultants and their clients. We've talked to people across a broad range of industries and locations. But most relevant here is that we've been able to gather data about leaders at a variety of different levels—from the presidents of multinational organizations to people who have no formal leadership titles. And in our collective experience, one of the biggest differentiators between those who are skilled leaders and those who are unskilled leaders, between those who are really leading and those who are leaders in name only, is their effort and ability to craft a compelling vision of where they want to take their groups.

Let's look at one study. We asked 3,574 people to rate a specific leader in their organizations and tell us if that person creates a strong vision for the group's future. At the same time, we were able to measure how well-regarded that person was as a leader. What do you think the relationship is between being a highly rated leader and crafting a strong vision? Take a look at Table 2.1.

Among the worst-rated leaders, hardly any crafted a strong vision for their groups. Presumably, they had other things to worry about. The story becomes a little more

Table 2.1. Ratings of Whether Leaders Create a Strong Vision for the Group's Future

Rating	Percent Who Do	Percent Who Don't
Best-Rated Leaders	87% do	*13% don't*
Middle-Rated Leaders	32% do	*68% don't*
Worst-Rated Leaders	10% do	*90% don't*

interesting, however, when we look at the middle group. If someone had set her sights on mediocrity, she wouldn't necessarily have to worry about the vision thing. Only about one-third of the people in this group created a strong vision for their people. So a leader can probably "get by" without having much skill in this area. No one's going to run you out of town. But what if you actually want high ratings as a leader? Well, 87 percent of the people in this group were able to put together a compelling vision for their groups. But why would this factor be such a differentiator?

If you're a leader, you're leading people somewhere else—somewhere that's not here. That's the job. If the group is staying in the same place, they may need a manager, but not a leader. Leadership is all about change. But change to what? That's why a vision is so important. The leader needs to have a crystal-clear vision of where the group is headed. What exactly will things look like when we pull this off? The leader needs to know the answer to this question—whether he's the CEO or the team supervisor.

When leaders lack a clear vision of the group's future, they are feeling their way through the execution process, relying on day-to-day revelations. Sure, they have a collection of goals, plans, and schedules, but they don't see the underlying tapestry, how everything fits together. They're much less likely to realize when priorities are misplaced or when opportunities are passing them by.

Vision, however, is about more than just the efficient use of time and resources. A truly great vision elevates our work. It sparks our imaginations. It touches on our human need to do something of value with our lives. Think of the difference between a beaver building a dam based on its instincts and a team of people building the Hoover Dam.

The vision of the Hoover Dam involved reimagining not just a river but an entire landscape. That vision opened up a whole awe-inspiring array of possibilities for the land and the community.

Visions are designed to inspire us. As we described earlier, a vision speaks to something that is uniquely human. If we list the contributions of a strong vision, we quickly recognize that they are uplifting in nature:

1. A vision can help us stand out from our competitors. Without a vision, Zappos might have taken the same road as other internet retailers, focusing on selection or price. Instead, CEO Tony Hsieh started with a vision of *Delivering Happiness*, as the title of his best-selling book indicates. A powerful vision can help everyone understand how whatever you do is differentiated from what your competitors do.

2. A vision provides purpose. Jim Collins, author of the business classic *Good to Great*, colorfully characterizes a vision as a BHAG (pronounced *bee-hag*, short for "Big Hairy Audacious Goal"): "A BHAG serves as a unifying focal point of effort, galvanizing people and creating team spirit as people strive toward a finish line." If you've ever been part of an energized team, whether around a conference room table or on a playing field, you know the feeling of pulling together to reach a common goal: suddenly everyone's work becomes essential and meaningful.

3. A vision drives the creation of goals. As baseball manager Yogi Berra famously noted, "If you don't know where you're going, you'll end up someplace else." When an organization or team is clear on the ultimate destination and the vision of that destination is firmly in mind, it's much easier to identify the necessary milestones to get there.

After you've read this list, think back to our study. The average leaders weren't crafting a strong vision and, as a result, they weren't getting the type of benefits listed above. This makes sense. After all, the group can probably get by even if it is a bit short-sighted or lacks a larger sense of purpose. But to be a truly great leader, you *will* need to use vision to elevate your group's work.

Vision at All Levels

Now, as the experienced leaders in our study remind us, vision is every leader's business, no matter where you fall in the hierarchy. We're stressing this point because it's one of the most commonly misunderstood aspects of leadership. When we speak to organizations about vision, we usually hear, "Crafting a vision needs to come from the top." We tell them, "Yes, *and* . . . at every level below it as well." After the top-level leaders craft a vision, then it's the responsibility of leaders at all levels to craft a vision for their teams supporting that top-level, organizational vision. And at each level, vision is equally important and must be well-crafted and appropriately communicated. As an example, your CEO's vision for the organization may be, "We will shift from domestic leader to international leader in the industry within five years." A customer service manager within the same organization might establish the following vision, which clearly supports the organization's vision: "To ensure our company is viewed as an international leader, we will offer 24/7 support in the local languages of all our customers." Both the CEO and the customer service manager are doing the Work of Leaders: crafting a vision.

Think of it this way: It's like a set of Matryoshka, those Russian nesting toys. In order for one to fit inside the other, they have to be similar shapes. Like nesting toys, a division leader's vision must support the organization's vision, but be relevant for her division. A department leader's vision must support the division, and so on.

And crafting a vision needn't stop there. Every member on your team can be encouraged to develop his or her own vision. As Peter Senge, author of the acclaimed *The Fifth Discipline,* observes, "Organizations intent on building shared visions continually encourage members to develop their personal visions. If people don't have their own vision, all they can do is sign up for someone else's. The result is compliance, never commitment."

In this view, vision is not a one-time event simply to be decreed and acted on until the next vision is delivered from on high. Rather, *crafting a vision is a dynamic, fluid, living process within an organization or team that benefits from multiple perspectives.*

So now that we've established why vision is so important, we'll use the next three chapters to explain how Exploration, Boldness, and Testing Assumptions can help you successfully craft a vision.

3

- Exploration
- Boldness
- Testing Assumptions

Execution

Crafting a Vision Through Exploration

We shall not cease from exploration, and the end of all our exploring will be to arrive where we started and know the place for the first time.
—T.S. ELIOT

A six-month-old will put just about anything in her mouth. If it fits, it's going in. A cell phone? *Looks good.* A stapler? *Hand it over.* A toner cartridge? *You mean I could have been sucking on this the whole time?!* She's exploring her world. Per square millimeter, there are more nerve endings in her mouth right now than in any other part of her body. Of course, as we grow older, our research is a little less reliant on our gums, but we're still a remarkably curious species. We try new restaurants. We tour houses we clearly can't afford. And yet, something unfortunate happens when we walk into the office on Monday morning. That sense of exploration takes a pretty serious dive. Why? Because we have plans and goals. We have obligations, commitments, meetings, an inbox full of email—you name it. Curiosity is one of the first casualties of responsibility.

When we ask leaders why they don't spend more time finding new opportunities for their groups, that's exactly what they tell us. Of the leaders who had a specific reason to give, 72 percent told us, "There's not enough time in the day." Not having enough time was, by far, the number one explanation. Interestingly, though, only 7 percent of leaders said that finding new opportunities wasn't part of their job. So we *know* that this is part of our role, but it's a "kinda-sorta" responsibility. Unlike all those other concrete tasks that are waiting for us, this one's murky. We know that we'll be held accountable for the concrete stuff, but if the exploration falls to the wayside—*well, you know, things happen.*

After all, finding new opportunities couldn't be *that* important. Otherwise, someone would have been more explicit about it. Right? That's not the picture our research paints. One of our studies offered 81,943 people the chance to give their leaders feedback. Table 3.1 shows the most common requests that people made.

Not only was finding new opportunities the most common request, but almost half of all people surveyed told their leaders to be more active about it. Even leaders who scored high in most other areas received this feedback.

Table 3.1. Most Common Requests for Leaders

I wish my leader would . . .	Percent of Raters Making Request
Be more active about finding new opportunities	47
Focus more on improving our methods	46
Do more to rally people to achieve goals	46
Do more to encourage the group to stretch the boundaries	45
Be more open to input from others	41

Further, the requests came from all directions—managers, peers, and direct reports.

What exactly are people asking for? They want their leaders to broaden the scope of the group's options, to look beyond the here-and-now. To uncover possibilities, both hidden and obvious. To explore the "What if's." *What if we teamed up with the London office? What if the two systems could talk to each other? What if we went paperless?* Not every direction is going to be a good one, but this is just exploration. It's about taking time to step back and think beyond the normal constraints that we unknowingly put on ourselves.

Of course, we realize that some people live for new opportunities. They take big gambles. They start new businesses. They pioneer new industries. But, as the study we mentioned earlier suggests, most of us probably don't fall into this category. And that's okay. The real key to exploration is making it a priority. Luckily, that's something we have at least some control over, no matter how tight our schedules.

If you're ready to commit some energy to finding new opportunities, there are two specific disciplines that will help you make the most of your time and effort. They are *remaining open* and *prioritizing the big picture*. We'll start with remaining open.

Exploration
▶ Remaining Open

Imagine you have a niece or sister or good family friend who is just starting her first year of college. She went into school undecided, but after her first semester, that's all changed. She just finished Introduction to Political Science. Her eyes have been opened for the first time. She can see now why people stand in line to vote. She finally understands why liberals and conservatives don't like to share a cab. Her plan? She's declaring her major and signing up for all poli-sci classes next semester.

What's your advice? Do you think she's ready to "tie the knot" with political science? Most of us would probably advise her to keep her options open for just a little bit longer and do some exploring. And while this might be obvious advice to give our young friend, when we find ourselves in leadership positions, many of us are less inclined to remain open to the possibilities ourselves. We're under pressure to make decisions and execute. We have to get results. In fact, when we ask leaders which task is more difficult, remaining open or gaining closure, the bigger challenge is clearly remaining open (see Table 3.2).

Table 3.2. Difficulty of Remaining Open Versus Seeking Closure for Leaders

As a leader, which of the following do you find *more difficult*?	
65%	Making sure I remain open to all possibilities without closing off my options too quickly
35%	Closing off options so that we have a clear direction

For many of us, the pleasure centers of the brain absolutely light up when we check something off our lists. Maybe not cookie-dough-ice-cream pleasure, but our neurons are wired to reward closure. More important here, however, is that some of us crave closure more than others do. Psychologists measure something called "need for closure." They even gave it an acronym (NFC). This need is defined as "a desire for a quick, firm answer (any answer) to a question." It's about a need to get rid of the uncertainty and ambiguity of not knowing.

Now, there are some real advantages to being a high-NFC person, such as being more structured and more likely to have a plan. They want to know that there's a clear path to the closure they dream about. In organizations, these are obviously highly desirable qualities. And as our research suggests, many people in leadership positions probably have some strong NFC tendencies. But when it comes to exploration, they may be at a bit of a disadvantage.

When you have a strong need for closure, you're much more likely to run with the first good idea or solution that you generate. A study by Arne Roets and Alain van Hiel confirms that high-NFC people actually show increased blood pressure and other autonomic symptoms when things are left up in the air. Consciously or unconsciously, you want to get rid of that stress. But like the college freshman, you put yourself in danger of settling early on an acceptable vision rather than one that is a truly good fit.

Remaining open doesn't mean you're indecisive. It's about making a conscious decision to invest time in exploration. It's not that you can't make up your mind—it's about not making a decision *too early*.

So, how do you resist the siren call of closure?

Strategies for Remaining Open

First, give yourself permission to set aside some specific time to let your mind wander, to think about the possibilities. Read an article or watch an online TED talk, and then take some time to figure out how it could connect back to your work. Remind yourself that it's okay if you don't have a tangible outcome every time. Have faith in the process—form a habit and give it time to pay off.

Next, resist the temptation to run with the first acceptable idea you generate. When we study people who are naturally good at remaining open, there are some striking similarities. Most noticeably, they allow themselves time to simply toy with an idea. They mull it over, look at it sideways, inside out, and upside down. They think about it in the shower. They mention it to colleagues, friends, even the doorman, and gauge their reactions. All the while they are trying to make connections and see the idea in new ways. Brain research shows that your mind is still working on problems even when you're not consciously thinking about them. This is why it's so important to give the process time.

Finally, don't reject an idea just because you aren't sure how it will be implemented. Being caught up in the logistics at this point can keep you from exploring a full range of possibilities. Remember that there will be plenty of time for planning and problem solving later.

ision
Exploration
▶ Prioritizing the Big Picture

For most of us, it's much easier to put together a puzzle if we use the picture on the front of the box as a guide. That's the big picture, literally. As leaders, of course, there's usually no obvious equivalent of the box. We have to imagine what the big picture will look like with all the pieces fitting nicely together. This shouldn't be too difficult, since we are dealing with something we do every day. However, it's usually more challenging than it sounds if we take the time to do it well.

The essential importance of seeing the big picture was popularized by Theodore Levitt in perhaps the most famous marketing paper ever published in the *Harvard Business Review*. In "Marketing Myopia" Levitt proposed that the central question companies must answer is "What business are you in?" He illustrated his point by demonstrating the consequences of railroad executives defining their business as railroads, instead of transportation. The inferences at the time were undeniable, as in the 1950s railroads were clearly losing their prominence as a means of moving people.

Although "Marketing Myopia" has stood the test of time, today there are other fundamental questions leaders should consider when defining the big picture. The most straightforward and useful we know of are the "Six

Critical Questions" in Patrick Lencioni's book, *The Advantage*. Lencioni's six questions for leaders are

1. *Why do we exist?*
2. *How do we behave?*
3. *What do we do?*
4. *How will we succeed?*
5. *What is most important, right now?*
6. *Who must do what?*

It's nearly impossible to imagine following the process Lencioni lays out without it resulting in a crystal-clear understanding of your organization's big picture. And the payoff for your work is just as certain. An insight into any one of these questions could very well spark the recognition of an opportunity. In turn, this opportunity could serve as the foundation for your vision.

The more clarity you have about how the pieces of your world fit together and interact, the more obvious your opportunities will be. Remember, this is the single most requested behavior change for leaders—"be more active about finding new opportunities." And that's what exploration is all about.

Strategies for Prioritizing the Big Picture

First, remember that a clear view of the big picture is only possible when you understand your context. Spend time outside your day-to-day responsibilities. Talk to your customers. Talk to your customers' customers. Talk to other teams in other departments. Talk to vendors. Ask any of these people about their experience working with your organization. What changes are they excited about? What are their frustrations? What are their pressure points?

Once you have a grasp of how the outside world sees your team or organization, spend time with your group defining your own big picture. Consider using Lencioni's "Six Critical Questions" as a starting point. Then, routinely ask yourself and your group broad questions like, "What factors are having the biggest impact on our productivity?," "What factors impact how well our group and this other group function together?," or "How does this particular activity contribute to our overall success?" Learn to resist the temptation to shut down conceptual conversations as a waste of time. You're developing theories that explain how your world works and why it doesn't always work as well as it should.

Finally, you can avoid becoming bogged down in the details by creating a list of potential problems and concerns. By putting the details in a "parking lot" and then setting it aside, you'll have more freedom to explore the big picture now and have the security of knowing you'll have a chance to deal with the particulars later. In fact, as you continue to explore the idea, many of the concerns might work themselves out anyway.

Tips for Exploration

- Set aside specific time for open-ended exploration.
- Give ideas a chance to percolate instead of pushing ahead with your initial thoughts.
- Remember that there will be time for planning and problem solving later.
- Look outside your group or organization to understand your context.
- Ask critical questions that help define the big picture for your group.
- Put the details in a "parking lot" to deal with later.

ision
Exploration
Boldness
Testing Assumptions

lignment

xecution

Crafting a Vision Through Boldness

People who don't take risks generally make about two big mistakes a year. People who do take risks generally make about two big mistakes a year.
—PETER DRUCKER

For decades, Sears, Digital Equipment, and Xerox colored inside the lines. That was the mistake. As Clayton Christensen chronicles in his classic book, *The Innovator's Dilemma,* these companies saw the end of their heydays because they failed to push themselves beyond the status quo. They were once viewed as very bold companies, but innovation seemed to stop as their successes grew. Of course, it's easy to see the evolution of a business in hindsight. But without a time machine, how can leaders know exactly when it's time to push beyond their current practices and established models? They can't. Not with certainty. And this is precisely why organizations need leaders who can craft a bold vision.

Most of us realize the world is constantly changing, and the pace of that change is growing faster. As a consequence, the lifespans of businesses are growing shorter. If leaders don't advocate for bold visions, we slowly become less and less relevant. This is why leaders at all levels need to show courage. As you can imagine, this comes easier to some of us than for others.

Why is boldness so difficult? Shouldn't we simply be able to spot the need for change and do it? We were curious, so we asked a sample of leaders, "What keeps leaders in your organization from being more bold?" Table 4.1 shows the responses of the people who had a specific reason to give.

First, we want to note that only 13 percent of people said that their organization didn't value boldness. In fact, in a separate question, over 76 percent of leaders said that it was somewhat important or very important to be seen as a bold leader in their organizations. So a lack of boldness on our part probably isn't due to a lack of interest from the organization. What is holding us back then?

Any time you're stretching the boundaries, there will be some resistance. As the results in Table 4.1 suggest, "People don't like disruption and change." It's human nature to seek out consistency and security. But ask those in the United States who had "secure" jobs in manufacturing how secure they feel now that their jobs have been moved overseas. In the VAE model, the effective leader understands that a

Table 4.1. Leaders' Reasons for Not Being Bold

What keeps leaders in your organization from being more bold?	Percent of Leaders Citing This Reason
People don't like disruption and change	52
Boldness is uncomfortable	30
Most leaders don't have enough power to be bold	22
Boldness can open you up to failure	19
It's just not worth it—it's too risky if we make mistakes	17
The organization doesn't value boldness	13

disruption to stability is sometimes necessary for growth (or even survival).

There's also a second story to be told from these results. Boldness is uncomfortable, opening the door to failure, blame, and criticism. By definition, success is not guaranteed. Not only are you taking a chance that you could fail, but you're putting other people's time and effort at risk. Think about this—if you are being appropriately bold as a leader, you *will*, in fact, fail occasionally. Put that way, boldness doesn't sound very tempting, does it?

And yet, if we take sanctuary in established rules and customs, our impact as leaders is limited. If a leader is not able to muster an inner spirit of boldness, it limits his ability to move forward.

For many of us, being bold means being outside our comfort zones. However, it need not be overwhelming. Broadly speaking, there are two components to boldness. The first is *being adventurous*, or envisioning a future that stretches the boundaries. The second is *speaking out*, or stepping up to promote that bold vision. Let's start with being adventurous.

Boldness

▶ Being Adventurous

Try to picture the world before maps. It might not be easy, since maps go back to about 12,000 B.C. Now, fast-forward about 14,000 years. Smart phones have map apps, cars have in-dash GPS—maps are everywhere. But where did all these maps come from? What kinds of people ventured into previously uncharted territory? Who goes where no person has gone before?

These are the adventurous leaders—people who set out to stretch the boundaries beyond what is currently known. They take chances in hopes of discovering a better world that isn't on our maps—yet. In fact, in some ways, an adventurous leader is the mapmaker.

Despite the seeming grandeur of this image, being adventurous at work is usually much more down-to-earth. Imagine a human resources director in a medium-sized organization. She knows that managers throughout the company spend hours a week doing paperwork, but she has a vision of a nimble organization. Her bold initiative is to eliminate some mandatory HR forms and merge others. How is this adventurous? It's a major disruption. Someone designed those forms for a reason, and that person is likely to push back. In fact, it may be like moving mountains to pull it off. She's facing a lot of uncertainty and unknowns.

Or imagine a manager in a large call center who has 60 percent turnover every year. His vision is to create a workplace that's not just adequate, but actually enjoyable—a place people brag about. He has a bold idea of introducing flex time. How is this adventurous? The organization currently prides itself on standardization and predictability, not flexibility. The idea has the potential of being a scheduling nightmare. And yet, he's willing to push forward because he knows it's what the department needs.

Unfortunately, only a fraction of the leaders we've studied describe themselves as highly adventurous. Meanwhile, "Do more to help us stretch the boundaries" is one of the most common requests we hear people give their leaders. And it comes from every direction—from the leader's manager, peers, and direct reports.

This tension between the nature of so many leaders to "play it safe" and the needs of their teams for help in stretching the boundaries is precisely why leaders must make a conscious effort to be more adventurous.

Strategies for Being Adventurous

How can you work more of a spirit of adventure into your leadership? Start by creating a good, old-fashioned list that weighs the pros and cons. Push yourself to imagine what would happen if you were to implement an adventurous design. Ask yourself: *What's the worst thing that could happen? What's the best?* Once you have identified your biggest fear, challenge yourself to confront it. What would happen if you overlooked the biggest "cons" in favor of the biggest "pros"?

Next, consider that being adventurous can have the added benefit of providing an opportunity to demonstrate your confidence in the group's abilities. People tend to live up to expectations, and this is a chance to describe the bold vision as a challenge to show them that you think they're up to it.

Finally, understand that you don't have to go it alone. Ideas don't happen in isolation, and they're often implemented by others. This is why, as you begin to move forward, it's important to start bringing others on board with your bold vision. This creates an opportunity to share responsibility with the people around you.

ision
Boldness
▶ Speaking Out

A psychologist who taught at the University of Minnesota liked to perform a simple in-class experiment with his students each semester. He'd ask them to guess how much time elapsed between hearing the words "start" and "stop." In the first trial, students wrote down their guesses on paper and handed them in. In the second trial, students reported their guesses out loud, one after another. Was there a difference between the two trials? Absolutely. When students guessed out loud, there was significantly less variability in the estimates. In other words, the students conformed—quite a bit. Out of the twelve times this little experiment was run, it never failed to produce pronounced conformity. And here's the kicker—the average private guess was almost always more accurate than the average public one.

The desire to not look like an idiot is woven into our DNA. In fact, people who don't have this instinct are much more likely to have some other type of psychological disturbance. It's normal, even healthy, to care about what others think of you. But this is one of the places in leadership where we need to rein in our self-protective instincts and push ourselves to go out on a limb, if that's what it takes.

Speaking out is voicing ideas that may seem unconventional or even impractical at first blush. It's the willingness to put your credibility on the line when a valuable idea is in danger of being swept under the rug. In fact, most bold ideas are born into a fragile existence. People quickly imagine all the ways this new idea will screw up their existing plans and processes. But if the leader's judgment tells her that this idea is truly worth considering, she has the responsibility to put herself out there and make sure it doesn't die prematurely. Bold ideas need a champion if they're ever going to have a chance.

Now perhaps the initial objections and fears will bear out. Maybe the idea requires too much risk or disruption. But in our experience, many of the knee-jerk objections to a bold idea are not quite as insurmountable as they seem at first. If the idea really is powerful, analysis and ingenuity can sometimes turn the impractical into: "You know, we might actually be able to do this." That realization, however, is never going to come to light if the leader doesn't have the strength to introduce it.

But for many of us, it takes a good deal of energy to stand firm against pushback. This is especially true when, just as you're putting forward your bold idea, someone steps in and says, "Let me play devil's advocate for a minute. . . . " Tom Kelley, general manager of IDEO and author of *The Ten Faces of Innovation*, believes that "the Devil's Advocate may be the biggest innovation killer in America today." We agree that it's a lot for any leader to stand up to. And yet, great leaders do precisely that because they know that a bold vision depends on them for survival.

Strategies for Speaking Out

Speaking out will certainly take more effort for some of us. Here are a few ideas to help you start.

First, remember that speaking out with a bold idea doesn't necessarily have to be done impulsively or on the spur of the moment. If it will help you build confidence, run your idea by one or two people you feel comfortable with before proposing it to a larger group. By pitching it informally, you'll gain a sense of how people are going to react and the opportunity to polish your delivery.

Second, don't apologize for your ideas or back down too quickly. Instead of saying, "I know this is a *bad* idea," say, "I know this is a *bold* idea." Infuse a little confidence into what you are saying instead of second-guessing yourself. You don't have to promote with absolute certainty, but the message is: "This is a really good opportunity and we owe it to the organization to figure out how to make it happen." Challenge people to put their skepticism aside for the moment. Instead of focusing on why this *can't* be done, focus on how it *can* be done. You can also reassure them that there will be other opportunities to revisit concerns that aren't addressed along the way.

Finally, you might as well plan for a little pushback so it won't throw you off track when it actually appears. Remember that people often need time to come around and a way to understand things on their own terms. And keep in mind that every idea doesn't have to succeed to make speaking out worthwhile. There will always be people who don't want change simply because it *is* change. But as a leader, it's part of your job to promote ideas that will make things better.

Tips for Boldness

- Make a list of pros and cons and focus on the benefits of the "pros."
- Show your confidence in the group by challenging them with a bold idea.
- Share responsibility for the bold vision with others around you.
- Gain confidence by first proposing your idea to people you feel comfortable with.
- Have a plan in place in case you find yourself intimidated by negative reactions.
- Assume you will have to deal with resistance.

5

ision
Exploration
Boldness
Testing Assumptions

lignment

xecution

Crafting a Vision Through Testing Assumptions

Most companies use research like a drunkard uses a lamppost: for support, not illumination.
—DAVID OGILVY

Have you ever fallen in love with an idea? If you have, you can probably remember the feeling. Eureka! You can't wait to tell the world what a cool idea you've come up with. You race to work to tell your boss, or home to dazzle your spouse, expecting to hear how brilliant you are. But instead, his nose scrunches up, and he might say something like, "I don't get it" or "That's interesting, but. . . . " And then tell you what you don't want to hear: it's confusing, it doesn't make sense, or it'll never work.

Okay, it's time to practice your deep breathing. What just happened? Your bold vision has just encountered its first reality check. It's time to ask yourself, "Is the idea not ready for the world, or is the world not ready for the idea?" Testing assumptions helps you bridge the difference between the two. And testing assumptions is the final driver of crafting a vision in the VAE model.

How likely are you to test your assumptions? Try this simple puzzle:

A bat and ball cost $1.10.
The bat costs one dollar more than the ball.
How much does the ball cost?

If you are like the thousands of college students who have answered the bat-and-ball puzzle, you probably didn't take much time to check your answer. Because a simple check will reveal that the most intuitive answer, which is 10 cents, is incorrect. (If the ball costs $.10 then the bat would have to cost $1.10, for a total cost of $1.20.) It takes most people a fair amount of trial and error to discover that the correct answer is 5 cents. But you can relax if you missed it because more than 80 percent of college students gave the wrong answer—including an astounding 50 percent of students at Harvard, MIT, and Princeton.

And as surprising as that seems, perhaps the most remarkable finding of this study by Nobel Prize–winning psychologist Daniel Kahneman and co-researcher Shane Frederick is that the reason most people answered incorrectly is that they failed to take the time to actively check their assumptions. In fact, Kahneman's recent book, *Thinking, Fast and Slow*, goes into great detail about why people are predictably prone to overconfidence when it comes to checking their intuition. And we all know how hard it can be to step back, especially once you've fallen in love with your idea.

But the good news is that, when we studied experienced leaders, we found a significantly higher percentage of people who understand the value of testing their assumptions. These seasoned leaders certainly have a wealth of wisdom packed in their heads, but part of that wisdom is recognizing the invaluable nature of multiple perspectives. They have learned how to use other people's reactions to the vision as a litmus test for what's in store as they work to bring it to life.

Still, testing assumptions may make you feel vulnerable. When you believe you've come up with something really good, your instincts are to protect it from criticism or rejection. And if you see asking for other people's opinions as wasting time, you aren't alone. About one in four leaders we studied claim there just isn't enough time in the day to ask for input.

But remember, the focus at this stage is on illumination. After your bold exploration, it's time to pause and estimate the odds before placing your bet. Consider it your due diligence. By understanding as much as possible about your vision, you'll be able to anticipate the potential reactions and challenges. You can't deal with problems you don't know about.

This doesn't have to be the "go, no-go" decision point. Instead, think of it as an opportunity to enhance, tweak, or understand the vision differently. Ultimately, it's about making the best decision you can by having the benefit of multiple perspectives.

So where do we begin when it's time to test our assumptions? In the VAE model, testing assumptions starts with *seeking counsel*.

Testing Assumptions
▶ Seeking Counsel

In an earlier time, we might have pictured a leader sitting in his big leather chair, making important decisions, then booming them out over the loudspeaker. Of course, this is an exaggeration, but leaders can miss a lot of good ideas if they never leave their offices. Seeking counsel is about inviting people whose skills and knowledge you respect into the process. This is your chance to try out your vision while the stakes are still low, to share your thoughts and gain new perspectives. It isn't asking someone for approval. The purpose is to find out what you don't know and to anticipate how the vision will unfold.

So how many people do you seek counsel from at work? Many of us carry around the prototypical image of the strong, independent leader who is thoroughly self-sufficient. She doesn't need an advisor, she is the advisor. And in fact, our research shows that this is the number one reason leaders don't seek counsel. Almost half the leaders we studied feel they are expected to make decisions on their own.

We also learned that almost 40 percent of leaders don't seek counsel because they prefer to trust their own instincts. We can relate. It might all make sense in your head, but other people will see things that you can't, or they might see things in a different way. Remember, the goal is to form a more complete picture. By gathering advice from people whose experience and knowledge you respect, you increase the likelihood of creating a vision that will work. There is no denying the advantage in hearing fresh perspectives—that's why the President has a cabinet.

Finally, asking someone to give you an honest opinion can be scary because you don't want to have someone poke holes in your idea. But if you know where the holes are, you'll be able to patch them up and your vision will be stronger. Consulting with others helps define your ideas more clearly. Seeking counsel also helps keep us humble and reminds us that we can never think of everything.

Strategies for Seeking Counsel

What if you're not used to seeking counsel or you don't have any go-to people to consult with?

First, to find your trusted advisors, take some time to observe the people you work with. It's not that you have to avoid people who never like anything or those who seem to say yes to everything. You just need to remember to consider the source. In fact, it might be useful to include some people at both ends of the spectrum to make sure you are considering a range of opinions.

Whenever possible, try to approach people individually rather than as a group so they don't influence each other, thus avoiding the well-known research artifact known as "groupthink." Engaging people in one-on-one conversations allows them to contribute their unique spins and explore their thoughts thoroughly and independently. Practice listening to their opinions without giving a rebuttal. Try asking, "What do you know that could disprove or support my assumptions?"

Finally, there's no reason to limit yourself to consulting with your co-workers. Consider other people you know who might have fresh perspectives that could be useful in refining your ideas, especially those closest to your customers.

Vision
Testing Assumptions
▶ Exploring Implications

Imagine what happens when you throw a smooth pebble into a still pond, setting off a seemingly endless ripple effect. Now picture what happens when you set your idea in motion in your organization. Same thing. But while the ripples in the pond are easy to predict, the effects of your idea as it moves out into the world are never as obvious. The goal in exploring implications is to imagine the effect the idea will have on your organization, from the first wave to the last ripple.

Who hasn't had an experience of hitting yourself in the forehead and saying, "How did we miss that?" Exploring implications is about thinking beyond the obvious, while at the same time not overlooking the obvious, like the roadblocks that often pop up along the way. Of course, there are always things you can't anticipate, but evaluating the vision thoroughly now could help save tremendous amounts of time and resources later.

But we all know what can happen. Sometimes the vision seems so clear, so compelling that it just feels perfect. It's easy to rush ahead when you're caught up in the excitement of a great idea. As Daniel Kahneman reminds us: ". . . when people believe a conclusion is true, they are also very likely to believe arguments that appear to support it, even when these arguments are unsound."

Strategies for Exploring Implications

The most common form of exploring implications is market research—describing an idea or showing a prototype to the intended users or audience. Even if this isn't something that your organization traditionally does, look at ways you can adapt the use of prototyping and concept testing to give your idea a more thorough examination. But caution should be exercised in not over-generalizing from qualitative research, such as focus groups. Remember, asking the opinions of a small group of people may be useful in exploring implications, but shouldn't be used to estimate the probability of success or failure.

Next, consider conducting a project "PreMortem," an exercise described by psychologist Gary Klein. The idea is based on a research study that showed that people's ability to predict a project's outcome improves by 30 percent merely by imagining that the event has already occurred, what the researchers called "prospective hindsight." Klein's PreMortem exercise consists of gathering a group of people in your organization and telling them that the project has failed spectacularly. You then instruct them to write down all possible reasons for the failure. Beyond the direct benefit of surfacing problems and implications while there is still time to make changes, Klein describes a number of advantages, ranging from making team members feel more valued to sensitizing the team to early warning signs of possible problems as the project starts rolling.

Finally, another way to use the power of the group was described more than one hundred years ago by Sir Francis Galton, a cousin of Charles Darwin and the statistician who created the statistical concept of correlation and the regression toward the mean. In 1907 Galton analyzed the data from contestants who estimated what the final weight of an ox at a livestock exhibition would be after it was slaughtered and dressed. Galton found that middlemost estimate (which we now call the median, not to be mistaken for the mean or average) of the 787 contestants was less than 1 percent off from the actual dressed weight of 1,207 pounds. The key is to ask an unbiased group of people to estimate the outcome, independently and privately, without any influence from the presenter or other group members. Probability suggests that the individual errors and biases will be cancelled out and the median is more likely to be predictive than any single estimate taken alone. So next time your team is sitting around a table debating an opportunity, consider having everyone take out a piece of paper and jot down a prediction. The median estimate may turn out to be your best guess.

Tips for Testing Assumptions

- Find people you trust to consult with, and reciprocate with them.
- Approach people individually rather than as a group.
- Look outside your group or organization to find fresh perspectives.
- Use marketing research with prototypes to test your ideas.
- Conduct a project "PreMortem."
- Have each group member make predictions about outcomes independently and use the median to estimate your chances of success.

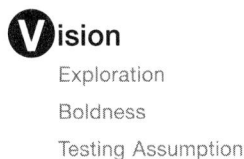
Exploration
Boldness
Testing Assumptions

Summary of Crafting a Vision

The first basic ingredient of leadership is a guiding vision. . . . Unless you know where you're going, and why, you cannot possibly get there.
—WARREN BENNIS

A few blocks from our San Francisco office sits what is arguably the most widely recognized building west of the Mississippi: the Transamerica Pyramid. Less well known is the story behind the design of this now world-famous landmark. It was commissioned by Jack Beckett, the CEO who led the transformation of his organization from a small,

53

obscure holding company into a Fortune 100 company that became a household name.

When plans for the futuristic skyscraper were first announced in 1968, the public reaction was overwhelmingly negative. Architectural critics howled. *Newsweek* magazine said the design would be "wrong in any city" but particularly wrong in San Francisco. *Progressive Architecture* magazine said it would be like "destroying the Grand Canyon." City officials were opposed. Neighbors were up in arms.

In the language of the VAE model, you might say that Beckett and his world-class architect William Pereira hadn't done a very good job of testing assumptions. But that's where the story takes a turn. Today, who can even imagine the San Francisco skyline without the Transamerica Pyramid? As one architect who had spoken against it at both hearings and rallies commented years later, "It's a wonderful building. And what makes it wonderful is everything we were objecting to." Today, we all know that Beckett's and Pereira's bold bet paid off.

So this is where the art of judgment comes in. VAE involves skills that can be learned and practiced—in this case, skills around exploration, boldness, and testing assumptions. But in the end, the leader has to apply judgment, asking herself how bold to be and how much to listen to critics and naysayers.

So how do the skills of crafting a vision fit into your world?

If you're in an executive leadership position, the answer to that question is perhaps obvious, since vision is likely part of your job description—whether stated explicitly or not. Leaders with this level of responsibility must set the aspirational course for the organization, painting the picture of a future that expands the view of what is possible, provides purpose, and drives the creation of specific goals. But remember: it's the work of leaders at all levels to craft a vision for their team that supports the organizational vision.

As you roll up your sleeves and prepare to do this work, use these tips and reminders to guide your process.

1. Choose the scope of the vision that fits your current leadership role and the needs of your group and organization. Take a moment to think about your sphere of influence as a leader. Are you accountable for enterprise-wide performance, your area or department's success, or that of your immediate work team? Who looks to you for direction and motivation? The level at which you function as a leader will determine the scope of the vision needed, from top-level ("We will be the most trusted provider of local moving services") to supporting ("To be the most trusted provider of local moving services, we will give customers the most timely and accurate estimates").

2. Find the right balance. This is where the art of using judgment comes in. You'll need to balance boldness and exploration with testing assumptions. Everyone's situation is different. Clearly, some industries and organizations have very little room for the risk that comes from a really bold vision. However, in those situations the leader can still be "bold"—it just may be about overcoming difficulties to create a meaningful change, rather than pursuing unproven and risky new ventures.

3. **Trust the process.** Remember that crafting a vision is a dynamic process that benefits from multiple perspectives. As such, it rarely follows a linear path. Parts of it may seem unfamiliar at first, and you may find it uncomfortable. The important thing is to be patient and stick with it. Make sure to set reasonable goals and expectations for yourself and your team. Don't forget to appreciate the milestones and to celebrate the clear vision that's essential to your long-term success.

Doing the Work: Crafting the Vision

Know the Scope of the Vision You're Crafting	
<ul><li>What is your sphere of influence?</li><li>At what level are you a leader in your organization?</li><li>Who looks to you for direction and motivation?</li><li>How will your vision relate to the larger organizational vision?</li></ul>	
Find the Right Balance	
<ul><li>How much exploration should you undertake?</li><li>What does boldness look like in your group, organization, or industry?</li><li>How will you determine the level of testing assumptions to pursue?</li></ul>	

Tips for Exploration

- Set aside specific time for open-ended exploration.
- Give ideas a chance to percolate instead of pushing ahead with your initial thoughts.
- Remember that there will be time for planning and problem solving later.
- Look outside your group or organization to understand your context.
- Ask critical questions that help define the big picture for your group.
- Put the details in a "parking lot" to deal with later.

Tips for Boldness

- Make a list of pros and cons and focus on the benefits of the "pros."
- Show your confidence in the group by challenging them with a bold idea.
- Share responsibility for the bold vision with others around you.
- Gain confidence by first proposing your idea to people you feel comfortable with.
- Have a plan in place in case you find yourself intimidated by negative reactions.
- Assume you will have to deal with resistance.

Tips for Testing Assumptions

- Find people you trust to consult with, and reciprocate with them.
- Approach people individually rather than as a group.
- Look outside your group or organization to find fresh perspectives.
- Use marketing research with prototypes to test your ideas.
- Conduct a project "PreMortem."
- Have each group member make predictions about outcomes independently and use the median to estimate your chances of success.

PART 2

7

Introduction to Building Alignment

The most empowering condition of all is when the entire organization is aligned with its mission, and people's passions and purpose are in synch with each other.
—Bill George and Peter Sims

We recently had a conversation with Nick, the talent sourcing manager for North America at a large manufacturing company with close to 100,000 employees in over thirty countries. He candidly shared with us the tough lesson he learned about the importance of alignment:

"The program I was in charge of introducing was great for the company, helping us control costs and streamline operations. I had the backing of the company president and of others above me. But it was going to mean a lot of change. Some people would see direct benefits; for others it would mean a lot of work and they wouldn't necessarily see the value personally.

"While it was a great vision, not everyone was on board. The people who actually had to do the work were pretty resistant.

"Well, long story short: the change never took place. Some of the stakeholders who couldn't see the worth of the program backed out. I was on vacation at a critical time, and while I was gone, the purchasing group called a halt to the whole project. It was a coup. People jumped ship."

Ouch. Nick's story makes it easy to see why building alignment really matters, because no matter how clearly you may see the picture of your improved future, without aligning others, your vision will remain a pipe dream.

What Exactly Do We Mean by Alignment?

Building alignment is the logical next stage after crafting a vision. Building alignment is the act of *gaining buy-in for your vision* and it's absolutely critical in moving from imagination to reality.

If crafting a vision is the most conceptual part of the VAE model, building alignment is the most people-centric and therefore is as complex and unpredictable as human relationships themselves. Yet, our research shows that more than half of leaders report little or no training or guidance in the practice of creating alignment. In fact, only 47 percent report having a clear understanding of what "building alignment" even means in the context of leadership.

The full spectrum of human motivations, personalities, cultural understandings, perspectives, and needs is present in your workplace every day. The people you work with may be seasoned veterans or new hires, with vastly different experiences and levels of responsibility. But building alignment means ensuring that each and every person understands his or her role in making the vision a reality.

Leaders who dread building alignment may think of it as "herding cats," unknowingly subscribing to a theory of human motivation developed in the 1960s by Douglas McGregor at MIT. In McGregor's Theory X, leaders assume that workers inherently dislike work, will show little ambition without enticement, and will avoid responsibility if possible. Theory X is about compliance rather than buy-in, with leaders preferring to have team members fall in line rather than align. Even if a leader doesn't hold such a disparaging view, his impatience and obsessive focus on the endgame may make alignment seem like a waste of time: "We have a vision, a direction, even a plan, so why aren't we doing it?"

On the other hand, effective leaders approach the process of building alignment via McGregor's Theory Y, assuming instead that employees are self-motivated, can solve problems creatively, and will exercise self-direction *if they are committed to objectives*. These leaders approach building alignment with deliberation, even passion. They know that it's going to take everyone's energy to make a vision happen.

Effective leaders also understand that alignment is not something to check off a to-do list. Alignment is a *dynamic, ongoing process* that requires continual monitoring and realigning as conditions and needs change. By staying plugged in, effective leaders can quickly tell when alignment begins to wane, and they can then give the time and energy needed to revive it.

Building alignment happens on both an emotional and a rational level. If you've ever flown on Southwest Airlines or shopped at Trader Joe's, you've probably witnessed this emotional component to alignment. People who work for these organizations clearly enjoy their jobs, and they go out of their way to make your experience something you want to tell your friends about. When a company's employees believe in a vision, you hear it in their voices and see it in their eyes. But, by itself, connecting with people emotionally is not enough to gain real buy-in. As Nick told us: "I'm really, really enthusiastic. And when the enthusiasm is catching, it feels like everybody's on board." But as he painfully learned, building alignment also means attending to the rational component: the need we all have to understand, to make sense of something before we commit to it. Nick explained that, in hindsight, "Maybe I didn't communicate enough of the details. Or I didn't communicate enough of what's in it for you." The members of Nick's purchasing group probably didn't *understand* the logic or see the value of the new company-wide program. Perhaps they also didn't *feel* personally rewarded or invested.

When both rational and emotional needs are met, when leaders reach the head *and* heart, true alignment goes beyond enthusiasm, beyond agreement, beyond understanding goals. True alignment changes the way team members view their actions; they embrace team decisions and organizational actions as if they were their own. As Seth Godin, author of *Tribes*, puts it, "The challenge for the leader is to help your tribe sing, whatever form that song takes."

Before we explore how to instill the passion, commitment, understanding, and motivation in others, let's look at why building alignment is so important.

The Importance of Building Alignment

Here are three reasons why building alignment is important to organizations and teams:

1. Alignment conserves time and energy. We all know the frustration of wasting time spinning our wheels or, worse yet, discovering that we've been going in the wrong direction altogether. The most effective leaders make sure everyone knows what they're supposed to be doing and why. Unfortunately, one in three leaders tell us they spend little to no time planning how they will achieve alignment. These leaders don't seem to realize that taking time for alignment is an investment that will pay for itself many times.

2. Alignment provides a forum for questions and concerns. A teacher in a major metropolitan public school system recently told us about a great plan her principal has to bring additional learning opportunities into the school by partnering with community organizations and businesses. Some of the teachers worry about how the program will be funded and sustained, while others are concerned about the time required to implement it. According to the teacher we talked to, however, that's not the problem. "She [the principal] won't take our questions!" she tells us. "Many of us actually think this is a good idea, but whenever we offer a refinement or ask her how it will work, she becomes defensive and takes it as a criticism. So now—most of us have washed our hands of it, essentially saying, 'Well, good luck with that.' It's a shame, really."

Because alignment opens the doors to healthy exchanges, it gives everyone in the organization or team an opportunity to feel a sense of ownership in the vision. Encouraging dialogue within organizations and teams is essential to gaining and maintaining buy-in; it is also an aspect of building alignment that some leaders fear the most. People need to feel that their concerns are understood and validated before they can move on. Leaders should recognize this need. Otherwise, they will be unable to gain traction to move toward executing the vision.

3. Alignment unites and excites people around a vision. When team members are unclear about the larger vision and don't feel personally invested, they can become demoralized, bored, or—as in Nick's case—may even mutiny out of frustration. Leaders who have successfully built alignment often recall the moment a vision took on a life of its own. Maybe it was when they first heard it discussed "around the water cooler." Or when they noticed the team working together with renewed energy and excitement, giving extra time and commitment. If Nick's co-workers had felt united around the new program and excited to help the entire company cut costs, Nick would have returned from his vacation to a much better homecoming.

Alignment at All Levels

Nick's tough lesson will make him a better leader, we're certain, because he sees the areas of improvement needed to become more successful at building alignment. He also recognizes one of the core principles of the VAE model: because leadership happens at all levels, building alignment also has to happen at all levels. It is the responsibility of each leader to gain buy-in across the organization. As Nick discovered, having the buy-in of the president didn't mean he had the buy-in of the team. He made the mistake of thinking the people at the top would push it down into the organization for him, but that didn't happen.

When we asked Nick what he'd do differently, he said that the experience has taught him to spend more time on building alignment. This is consistent with our research, which shows that the more experienced the leader, the more inclined he is to invest the energy it takes to align people around the vision.

In the next three chapters you'll learn how to use Clarity, Dialogue, and Inspiration to build both emotional and rational buy-in for a vision.

8

ision

lignment
Clarity
Dialogue
Inspiration

xecution

Building Alignment Through Clarity

Speak clearly, if you speak at all; carve every word before you let it fall.
—Oliver Wendell Holmes

We have a few favorite words around our office. One is *crisp*. It's the perfect word to describe clear leadership communication. When it's crisp, it provides enough information, but not too much. It is well-structured and efficient. It leaves followers with a clear image in their heads. But crisp can be really tough. In fact, it's an art. When we see a master communicator in action, it's almost impossible to appreciate the skill that's required to make a complex, highly involved message so elegant and simple. The good news is that your deliberate efforts in this area can lead to valuable returns on your investment.

Imagine a seemingly straightforward task, like describing the third movie in a trilogy to a group of people. How do you decide which elements of the plot to include? What details do you provide about each character? Do you mention the cool special effects? As you tell your story, you can't help but notice the looks on people's faces. Some of them get it. They probably saw the first two movies in the trilogy. Others look completely lost, and it's unclear how to keep them from zoning out. How can you make what only you have seen real to them?

Of course, describing a movie is usually nowhere near as challenging as painting a picture of something that doesn't even exist—a vision.

When we communicate about a future vision, plan, or change, it's easy for us to forget how little context other people have. After all, as the leader, you were probably involved in the decision-making process. You were able to (or had to) sit through all sorts of conversations during which ideas were batted around. You know the history that led to the decision being made the way it was. Our research suggests that leaders often overlook communicating what is obvious and intuitive to them, but can seem like a mystery to their followers. We tell them the outcomes, the decisions, without connecting the dots to the thinking behind the decisions. So, where do leaders commonly go wrong? Table 8.1 summarizes the most frequent comments that people gave their leaders when they needed more clarity.

Table 8.1. Comments Given to Leaders About Clarity

Comments (from Most to Least Frequent)
Sometimes he/she does not give enough detail to clarify what is expected.
There are times when he/she could better organize what he/she wants to say before communicating.
He/she sometimes assumes I already understand a difficult topic.
He/she tends to spend a lot of time on unnecessary details or unrelated tangents.
He/she doesn't seem to fully form his/her thoughts before communicating.
He/she rarely states the topic before he/she begins explaining his/her points.
He/she moves too fast for me to grasp what he's/she's talking about.

As you can see, this is where the art comes in. Providing clarity involves a delicate balance between keeping it simple and addressing real-world complexities. This means sharing enough specifics to anticipate basic questions without drowning the listener in details. You need to concisely describe the vision, explain the purpose behind it, and give the specifics of how it affects your audience.

Of course, it's not always as easy as knocking off one, two, and three. Each of us struggles with different aspects of providing clarity. For instance, leaders who are more private often prefer to communicate on a need-to-know basis. They dispense information in small bits and keep their office doors closed the rest of the time. On the other hand, talkative types can be so wordy that people have trouble picking out what's really important. Highly conceptual leaders tend to leave out important details. Highly concrete leaders often fail to pull the details together into a compelling big picture.

Regardless of your particular challenge, and we all have them, we want to offer two practices to help you boost your clarity: *explaining your rationale* and *structuring your message*. As simple as they seem, we find they are often overlooked.

lignment
Clarity
▶ Explaining Rationale

Here's a simple, now-famous experiment by Harvard researcher Ellen Langer. First, Langer approached people in a long line at a library photocopier and asked, "Excuse me, I have five pages. May I use the Xerox machine?" Sixty percent of people said yes. Next, Langer approached people and asked, "Excuse me, I have five pages. May I use the Xerox machine because I'm in a rush?" That was the difference, the simple addition of, "because I'm in a rush." So how much of a difference can just five words make? When the last clause was added, the number of "yes" responses went up to 94 percent. That's more than a 50 percent increase in persuading people to say yes to the exact same request.

Why in the world did this work? It worked because people respond to simple explanations. In this case, even a weak rationale made a huge difference. It turns out that the mere presence of an explanation is powerful on many levels. Think of it as the information behind the information. Now, most of the time, an explanation like "because I'm in a rush" won't really be enough. But if you're able to give a simple reason for a change or new plan, people should be able to follow your logic and reach the same conclusions.

Usually, the more unpopular or demanding a change is, the more important it is to give people a solid reason. Think of it this way: if your company suddenly decided to give everyone free lunches, people wouldn't need any more information to jump on board. On the other hand, if your company decided to take away free lunches, people would want to know why. It needs to make sense if you want them to follow you willingly.

Finally, there's one time in particular that explaining one's rationale is most important—in times of uncertainty or great change. Harry Kraemer, professor at the Kellogg School of Management, in his book *From Values to Action*, offers a simple, but powerful formula: Change + Uncertainty = Chaos. He goes on to describe the speculation and gossip that occur when leadership doesn't step in to offer clarity. If people aren't given explanations in a straightforward manner, they'll often unintentionally make them up. And once that process starts, it's tough to rein the group in. The solution? Be proactive. Over-clarify and over-communicate when the situation calls for it. You'll thank yourself later.

Strategies for Explaining Rationale

Once you realize how important this skill is, the question that begs to be answered is: *"How do I get there?"*

First, try this exercise. Sit down with a blank sheet of paper. Place a small circle at each end of the page. These are your "Point A" and "Point B." Label each point in ten words or less to explain where you are today and where you will be when you achieve your vision. Now, in between the two points, write the three most straightforward reasons you need to or you are choosing to move from "Point A" to "Point B." What you are aiming for here is *transparency*. When there's transparency in an organization, people at all levels feel they have access to essential information, and they're more likely to trust what you're saying. Consider the leadership experiment in which participants read about the CEO of a fictional company going through downsizing (Norman, Avolio, & Luthans, 2010). In one case (the transparency condition) they read a speech by the CEO that provided specific information and reasons for the downsizing. In the other case (the non-transparency condition), participants read an equally long speech, but it didn't include a thorough discussion of the reasons for the downsizing. Not only were the transparent CEOs rated as significantly more trustworthy, but they were also rated as much more effective leaders.

Next, work to shift perspectives and look at the situation from your listeners' point of view. Study after study shows that as a person's authority increases, her awareness of other peoples' needs diminishes. Think about it this way: you probably spend a lot more time monitoring your boss's mood than your boss spends monitoring your mood. So as a leader, make a deliberate effort to understand the concerns and fears of your group, then target your message to meet them where they are.

Finally, monitor people's reactions for comprehension. This is where you need to slow down, pay attention to body language, and read between the lines. If you sense confusion, take time to ferret out any areas of misunderstanding or uncertainty. You may not realize that information is missing or that there are disconnects, so you need to rely on the reactions of the group to know whether or not you are being clear.

Alignment
Clarity
▶ Structuring Messages

Now we come back to crisp. Crisp doesn't just happen on its own and it can be tempting to just ignore it. Why can't you just speak off-the-cuff? You have all the information—you'll put it out there, and if they have questions, they'll ask. You tell yourself, "I'm busy, and crisp takes time." But there is no easy way out if you want the benefits of clarity working for you. You have to take time to structure your message.

Think about how it feels to be handed a mess of information and be expected to figure it all out. Meandering, unfocused communication leaves people wondering whether the leader has his act together. On the other hand, well-structured messaging says, "Here's a person who knows where he's taking us."

Strategies for Structuring Messages

First, start by finding your "headline." If you can't boil it down to eight words, it's probably too complex to understand. Be sure to test it out on a couple of people to make sure it communicates what you're intending, and refine it as needed.

Next, nail down your talking points. The question to ask yourself is: "If people walk away with nothing else, what two or three points do I want them to remember?" Politicians are particularly good at this. They find the essence of the message and hit those "talking points" again and again. They've identified the specific elements that make the message simple and memorable. The part that often takes the most work is balancing the big picture and the details. Each case is different, but here are some questions to ask yourself when narrowing down your talking points:

- What is the most compelling reason why this new effort is being undertaken?
- What are the essential details?
- How can details be grouped together in a way that's simple and logical?
- What is the most down-to-earth way to describe how the group will benefit when it's all done?

Finally, once you've found your message, refer back to it often and consistently. The simple fact is that people tend to have more positive feelings about things they have been exposed to repeatedly. In 1968, University of Michigan psychologist Robert Zajonc began a series of landmark experiments showing that, contrary to the old saying, familiarity does not breed contempt. In fact, just the opposite is true. People's feelings, even toward nonsensical words, consistently grow more positive as their exposure increases. Zajonc's "mere exposure effect" has been reexamined and supported by dozens of other studies that show the importance of repetition and familiarity in shaping people's attitudes and feelings. The simple lesson for leaders is clear. Find your message and stick with it.

Tips for Clarity

- Be straightforward and transparent.
- Look at it from the listeners' point of view—it needs to make sense to them.
- Monitor people's reactions for comprehension.
- Find the "headline" of your message—you should be able to boil it down to eight words or fewer.
- Create talking points that balance the big picture and the details.
- Refer back to your message repeatedly over time.

Clarity
Dialogue
Inspiration

Building Alignment Through Dialogue

A dialogue is more than two monologues.
—Max M. Kampelman

Most of us wouldn't guess it, but there's actually an important difference between *discussion* and *dialogue*. In *The Fifth Discipline*, Peter Senge summarizes the origins of these words, explaining that "discussion" has the same root as the words percussion and concussion—"literally a heaving of ideas back and forth in a winner takes all competition." Dialogue, however, is much more subtle and sophisticated. It comes from the Greek word *dia-logos*. *Dia* means *through*, and *logos*

79

means *word* or *meaning*. Put together, the word suggests "a free-flowing of meaning through a group, allowing the group to discover insights not attainable individually."

Through dialogue, the leader establishes a two-way conversation, in contrast to the one-way communication needed for clarity, as described in the previous chapter. It involves suspending judgment and stretching to connect with the other person's point of view. This requires openness and active listening.

True dialogue goes beyond a simple communication check. Skilled leaders use dialogue as an opportunity to give people a voice. By engaging the group and making others part of the conversation, you open the door to shared ownership and accountability. In short, you gain buy-in and begin to build engagement.

However, it would be a mistake to think that the sole purpose of dialogue is engaging others. Effective leaders are aware of just how much value can be gleaned from the input of the people they lead. This awareness is supported by another core leadership trait—humility. Nowhere is the value of humility made clearer than in the process of dialogue. Humility allows leaders to benefit from other perspectives, because they realize they don't have a monopoly on insight. In fact, the people who are closer to the action often have the most practical, real-world knowledge. They help to solve problems or point out issues that would be hidden otherwise. A humble leader isn't paying lip service by asking for feedback, but instead she actually *wants* to know what people think.

Dialogue is an art, but it's also a skill that can be developed by practicing two key behaviors: *exchanging perspectives* and *being receptive*.

lignment
Dialogue
▶ Exchanging Perspectives

Several years ago we did a study to see what factors played the largest role in determining a person's happiness at work. When we asked, "Which of the following would greatly increase your job satisfaction?" it was a landslide. "Better pay" far surpassed every other factor. Not a huge surprise. But we're sneaky. We did a second study to see what is *actually* most correlated with current job satisfaction. In this study, pay was more than halfway down the list. That is, people *think* pay is going to make them more satisfied, but other variables end up being far more important. What are these other variables? The factor that had the highest correlation with job satisfaction was "a chance to have my opinions heard and considered." Not only is this leadership behavior much more powerful than pay, but it's something every organization can afford.

But let's put this in more concrete terms. Remember Nick from Chapter 7? Clearly, he had trouble aligning people. Perhaps he had a great idea, but the people who were supposed to execute it had significant reservations. His critical mistake? He never gave people an open forum to work through those reservations. He assumed the idea was so valuable that, with support from the top, it would eventually overcome lingering resistance when it came time to implement. But he was wrong.

If Nick had taken the time to give people a chance to have their opinions heard and considered, he might have headed off the eventual coup. If he had truly exchanged perspectives, he would have understood where others were coming from, made any necessary adjustments, and gained their trust and buy-in.

Obviously, we want the people we lead to *get it*—to share our vision, our plan, our urgency, our passion. But what we so often forget as leaders is that it's just as important for people to know that *we* get *them*. There's a whole lot of power in that little word "get." We all know what it's like to work with someone who gets us.

Think about the last time you were struggling to get your point across. It's a relief when the other person's face lights up with a look of understanding. You can almost see the light bulb appear as he nods enthusiastically and says, "Oh, yeah, I see what you mean." Even if he doesn't agree with you, he gets it—and that makes you feel good.

In many cases, once people feel understood, they can open up more about what's really bothering them. Maybe underneath all the reservations, people are worried about their workloads. Maybe they feel like the quality of their work will suffer. But maybe it's deeper, the kinds of things people don't readily admit. Perhaps they fear that their skill sets will be outdated, or their territory will be invaded. You don't have to be a therapist. You just have to be interested in where they're coming from. Listen and encourage them to share.

Patience is essential. It's important to let people meander and to give them enough space to find their meaning. Remember, they haven't had as much time as you to get their heads around these new ideas. They may not be as articulate as you are. And if you rush them to wrap it up, they probably will. But that doesn't mean you've heard what you needed to hear or that they'll be ready to follow.

If learning to exchange perspectives sounds like hard work, consider this. We asked more than 16,000 people to tell us about the leaders they enjoy working with most. The leaders who consistently rose to the top were those who genuinely listen to other people and take others' input and ideas seriously. So if you want to become a leader that people like to follow, you couldn't find a better place to start.

Strategies for Exchanging Perspectives

In our experience, exchanging perspectives can be extremely difficult for certain types of people. The classic Type A personality is tempted to keep moving and skip "all this fluffy stuff." On the other hand, we find many introverted, analytical leaders who are uncomfortable with conversations that are even remotely emotional in nature. Here are some reminders and strategies for those of us who don't naturally gravitate toward exchanging perspectives.

First, it's important to give people a safe place to open up. Create an environment that's relaxed and informal. Choose a time and place where people won't feel rushed or threatened. Ideally, visit them in their own workspace or a neutral space during a downtime.

Next, remember that there are advantages to exchanging perspectives one-on-one. While leadership involves leading a group or organization, gaining buy-in is sometimes best done at the individual level. Have you ever noticed the difference between the responses of people when they're alone versus in a group? This is known as the "audience effect." In a group, people may avoid speaking up or saying what they really think because of perceived threats or conformity to group norms. Noted psychologist Jacques

Lacan pointed out the importance of the "gaze of the audience" and how people's beliefs about their audience affect their behavior, including how they communicate and interact. In short, people are more likely to participate in a genuine exchange if they don't have to worry about the reactions of others around them.

Finally, practice reflective listening. This is a technique developed by therapists, but you don't have to be a therapist to use it. Simply put, it's about summarizing what someone said, using your own words. Not only does this assure that the speaker feels heard, but it forces you to listen more actively so you can feed back what you understood. You'll discover that, when you accurately and non-judgmentally summarize other people's messages, they will often take it as an invitation to dig deeper.

lignment
Dialogue
▶ Being Receptive

In a leadership interview, we heard about Alan, a quality director at a major American appliance manufacturer. He was an extremely sharp guy. He excelled at vision. Equally impressive, he could clearly see how things were going to be done. He had an instinct for spotting which processes were going to be most efficient. What was the problem? His department had a 50 percent turnover—people just didn't like working for him. It actually wasn't until they saw the exit interviews, his casualties, that senior leadership realized what was really going on. It turned out that this leader just issued orders without leaving room for discussion. More important, people felt steamrolled if they offered an opposing perspective. The general consensus among the group was to be extremely careful expressing opinions around Alan, especially if you disagreed with him. In fact, people pretty quickly learned that the wisest course of action was to keep your head down, do what you're told . . . and get out of there as soon as you could. There's nothing terribly shocking about this story, and that's the whole point. We've probably all been in a situation like this, which makes it easy to understand why it's so important to be receptive, and why it's a critical behavior in creating dialogue.

Being receptive is a bit more straightforward than exchanging perspectives. It's not so much about the process of having the conversation or even the content of the conversation. It's about the vibe you're sending out during the conversation. Both consciously and unconsciously, people sense whether you are receptive and approachable. We're not talking about Kumbaya here. You don't have to hold anyone's hand. But people do need to know that, even if they say something stupid, they're not going to be met with an eye roll.

Now all of this may sound like a no-brainer, but here's some real feedback we received when we asked people how good their bosses were at staying open to input:

- "He does ask for input and feedback, but doesn't really listen to or consider it."
- "She doesn't seem to feel that the opinions of others are important."
- "There are only a few people he listens to."
- "When input isn't positive, she is quick to dismiss further discussion."
- "He frequently shoots down others' ideas."

- "When the group is trying to come up with ideas or suggestions, she acts like she is being personally attacked."

Now we doubt anyone's going to read this passage and squeal, "That's me! That's me!" Indeed, these are some of the more extreme examples, but many of us leaders do, whether we know it or not, indulge in similar behaviors from time to time.

Over the last decade, we've measured the personalities of tens of thousands of leaders, and it's clear that many have moved into leadership positions by being driven and results-oriented. They're no-nonsense people, and challenging everything is second-nature to them. To be sure, these qualities offer some advantages for the individual and the organization. But results-oriented leaders are often those who struggle the most with the receptivity needed to gain alignment. It's really hard to be challenging and receptive at the same time.

In a nutshell, challenge kills vulnerability. In his best-selling *The Five Dysfunctions of a Team*, Patrick Lencioni demonstrates how powerful the use of vulnerability is in the development of a high-performing team. In Lencioni's workshops, teams are encouraged to build trust through a vulnerability exercise. Each person on the team shares a work-related weakness that other members may not know about. As you can imagine, this exercise isn't always met with enthusiasm. But by the end of the workshop, it's not uncommon for attendees to recall it as one of the most powerful activities of the day.

While the workshop offers a carefully crafted environment that makes it okay to be vulnerable, it's you as the leader who has to step up and set that tone for your team. When leaders encourage (or even reward) vulnerability, people can express their true doubts and concerns. They don't need to worry about how they'll be perceived. And perhaps most important, they don't have to worry about tap dancing around the leader's ego. By contrast, when vulnerability is absent, people protect their ideas and their territory. The group's plans and goals don't benefit from candid conversation because the interpersonal stakes are too high. To be sure, it takes a strong leader to move from challenge to the vulnerability required so that people feel heard.

Strategies for Being Receptive

If you're the kind of leader who leans more toward "It's my way or the highway" than roasting s'mores around a campfire with your co-workers, here are a few strategies to help you show more receptivity.

First, make sure your tone of voice and your body language verify your receptiveness. We all know that it's not what you say but how you say it that has the biggest impact. Remember, people can sense skepticism or disapproval, so try to suspend those feelings and encourage others to voice their concerns.

Next, don't immediately try to counter what someone else has said. Remind yourself that this is the time for openness, not debate. If you are focused on pushing back, you won't really be listening. Saying, "Tell me more about that" keeps the conversation going without being judgmental. Being receptive involves empathy and emotion, and it doesn't mean that you have to try to fix everything. Sometimes people just want to be heard.

Actively consider whether people are simply telling you what you want to hear. In such cases, the result will be compliance but not commitment. You'll see some head nods, even if it doesn't feel right to them. Look for questioning looks, furrowed eyebrows, even disinterest. This isn't a good start to aligning people, so do your best to set the stage for an honest dialogue and provide enough time to make sure people have the opportunity to say what they want to say. In some cases, you may need to sit down with people individually to give them the chance to really express what they're thinking.

Tips for Dialogue

- Create an open and relaxed environment.
- Have one-on-one conversations with people.
- Practice reflective listening.
- Make sure your tone of voice and body language come across as receptive.
- Be careful not to debate or battle for your own side.
- Look for signs of people just telling you what you want to hear; then encourage more honest feedback.

10

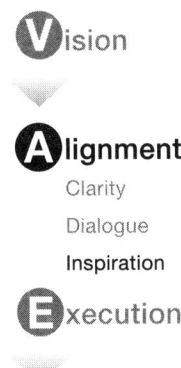

Vision

Alignment
Clarity
Dialogue
Inspiration

Execution

Building Alignment Through Inspiration

If you want to build a ship, don't drum up people to collect wood and don't assign them tasks and work, but rather teach them to long for the endless immensity of the sea.
—Antoine de Sainte-Exupery

Are you inspiring? Where would you rate yourself on a 5-point scale? We asked 13,000 people this question and fewer than one in five gave themselves a top score. Even more telling was how people rated themselves on a list of other adjectives associated with inspirational leadership (see Table 10.1).

89

Table 10.1. Self-Ratings on Adjectives Associated with Inspiration

Adjective	Percent of People Who Give Themselves a Top Rating
Compelling	5.8
Captivating	8.1
Magnetic	11.0
Stimulating	12.2
Dynamic	12.9

The data tell a clear story. It's only a select group of people who see inspiration as their thing. And for most of us, someone telling us to be more inspirational is like telling us to be taller. It doesn't feel like something we really can change. Fortunately, that's not necessarily true. Inspiration may take a little more deliberate effort for those of us who aren't naturally captivating and magnetic, but it certainly is something we have control over. What we want to do in this chapter is break down the inspiration mystique and show how every leader can harness its power to gain alignment.

Like dialogue, inspiration helps leaders gain buy-in. Instead of focusing on empathy and understanding, however, the goal here is to breathe life into the vision so that people are galvanized and become emotionally committed. It goes beyond a well-constructed logical argument—it's about painting an exciting picture of the future. This image of a leader inspiring a team is almost synonymous with leadership. And yet, our research suggests that this is one of the areas leaders neglect the most.

When we asked people to give their leaders feedback, almost half of them requested that their leaders "do more to rally people to achieve goals." What was even more interesting was the difference between how leaders rate themselves and how their followers rate them. We found that leaders tend to see themselves as significantly better at rallying people than their followers see them. Not surprisingly, the leaders who receive this request most often are the ones with reserved or analytical styles. But there are ways to rally people that don't involve using a megaphone.

Once you understand what's really at play, you might realize you have some of it in you after all. When we break inspiration down to its essence, we're talking about bringing positive energy to your group and your goals. In the VAE model, there are two components that help with this: *being expressive* (the energy) and *being encouraging* (the positivity). Another way to think of it: You're sending people a message that says, "*You matter* and *this matters.*"

Inspiration
▶ Being Expressive

Have you ever read a work of poetry and felt moved by it? Perhaps you're not a poetry person—but what about an article, a book, or a simple passage of text? Many people find inspiration in writing, and the source of inspiration exists in the words. And it doesn't just appear when read aloud by a dynamic speaker. The words and ideas themselves are just as profound when we read them silently to ourselves. The writer has found a way to communicate his or her passion in a way that connects to the audience. This is what we mean by being *expressive.*

As this example shows, being expressive isn't the same as being loud. You can create energy without bouncing off the walls. What's important is conveying your thoughts or feelings in a way that reaches people on an emotional level. If you're passionate about your work (and a leader must be), you have any number of options for expressing that enthusiasm. A naturally expressive leader may communicate her passion spontaneously. A high-energy leader may create an event that serves as a pep rally. But even the most reserved leader can find a way to express and instill genuine feeling.

In fact, sometimes the quietest people engage in the most in-depth thinking about their goals. If you have a handle on why your work is important, you're halfway there. The next step is putting it into words and sharing a sense of purpose with the group. Crafting a picture of how amazing things will be when the team reaches its goals creates a positive energy. Being expressive isn't grandstanding or hollow charm. It's believing in the vision and helping people see the real, deeper meaning behind their tasks. It's part of your job as a leader to express belief in the eventual outcome, to transmit that sense of importance.

Strategies for Being Expressive

For some of us, sharing excitement and enthusiasm often happens without any effort at all. In fact, sometimes we don't even know we're doing it. But for those of us who don't wear our hearts on our sleeves, here are some strategies to help.

First, you need to be clear in your own mind why you're passionate about the vision. Before you express your thoughts, really think about how you're feeling and put a label on it. Why are you genuinely excited about the goal or vision? Paint an irresistible picture for yourself. By connecting with your emotions, it will be easier for you to convey your optimism.

Next, be specific. Try using the talking point strategy from Chapter 8, except this time choose three points that speak more to people's hearts than to their heads. Answer the question: "What three things will we feel best about when we successfully achieve our vision?" Be authentic and real, and people will be able to connect with what you're saying. The key is to tie specific results back to a big picture that you're asking everyone to invest in.

Finally, remember that, just as when you communicate for clarity, your body language and mood may speak louder than your words. In his book *Primal Leadership*, Daniel Goleman, a pioneer in the area of emotional intelligence, describes how the leader-follower relationship is hard-coded in our brains. He explains the tendency of employees to perceive the business environment through the eyes of their leaders. In other words, the moods, opinions, and actions of leaders rub off on their followers. On a very basic, unconscious level, people internalize and reflect the same feelings put forth by the leader. If you come across as cynical, unsure, or pessimistic, it will be mirrored by the group. On the flip side, if you convey an upbeat optimism, your followers will likely do the same; if you appear excited and committed to the vision, your followers will be, too.

Alignment
Inspiration
▶ Being Encouraging

Noted research psychologist John Gottman has created some truly remarkable models to predict the success of a marriage. By analyzing a three-minute video clip of spouses talking to each other, he is able to predict whether they will stay together with over 90 percent accuracy. Pretty impressive. Makes you wonder how you would do. Here's a hint: a lot of it is about the ratio of positive exchanges to negative exchanges. Healthy couples in his research have a five to one ratio of positive to negative. What does this have to do with leadership? Well, leadership is also about relationships, and a lot of the same emotional mechanisms are at play in the work arena. So it's worth asking yourself: How often do you deliver five positive messages to every negative? Nobody's going to divorce you at the office, and maybe they won't even quit—but more likely, if the relationship goes sour, you'll gradually lose their commitment to their work. People need encouragement, and it must be ongoing.

By definition, being encouraging means giving support, confidence, or hope to someone. The goal is to make people feel good about the work they're doing, the team they belong to, and the goal they're aiming for. It's important to distinguish this from giving feedback, which we'll discuss in Chapter 15. Giving positive feedback is reactive, but giving encouragement is proactive. We are telling people that we believe in them and that we *will* succeed. And by giving this sort of support up-front, people will be more likely to feel like they matter and align with the vision.

When you think of all the sources of negativity that can creep into the work environment (setbacks, delays, complaining, arguments, or criticism), someone should be infusing positivity into the situation. The leader is that someone. In his book, *The One Thing You Need to Know*, Marcus Buckingham pegs the opposite of a leader as a pessimist: "When I say leaders are optimistic I mean simply that nothing—not their mood, not the reasoned arguments of others, not the bleak conditions of the present—nothing can undermine their faith that things will get better." Here we're talking about something even more fundamental than the outward encouragement of a leader. We're talking about the leader's core outlook.

But for some of us, being too optimistic might feel like we're putting our credibility on the line or making ourselves vulnerable to cynicism and possible failure. After all, if you present yourself as a realist, you can hedge your bets in a way. You don't have to worry that someone will come to you and say, "Hey! You said this was going to happen and it didn't!" Furthermore, for some of us, remaining matter-of-fact feels more dignified, more controlled, more business-like. What experience and research tell us, however, is that it's necessary to give up some of that emotional safety as a leader. It can be tough, but showing optimism and hope is a crucial part of gaining alignment.

Strategies for Being Encouraging

First, give people a common aspiration, something that the whole group can latch onto and be inspired by. There are lots of ways to do this. A traditional strategy is identifying a "common enemy." Buried deep in our DNA is an "us versus them" mentality. But as the authors of the book *Tribal Leadership* explain, even better is moving beyond this competitive mindset to seek out a set of common values and use them to define a "noble cause." In their words, "If core values are the fuel of a tribe, a noble cause is the direction where it's headed. A noble cause captures the tribe's ultimate aspiration."

Next, consider adding a rallying cry, built on your common aspiration. You can think of this as a marketing slogan that you use internally. Like all marketing, make it clear, simple, and easy to remember. For example, one of us had a job right out of business school at a consumer products company that had a rallying cry of "25 in '89." Having struggled to increase market share for more than a decade, the organization set an ambitious goal of reaching 25 percent market share by 1989. It was a constant reminder that *hey, we're in this together, and we can do it!* It was a stretch, but the company pulled it off.

Finally, consider your audience. One of our colleagues admitted to the following story. He was the head of a department speaking to a couple hundred employees about the group's recent success. His intention was to get everyone jazzed up and inspired by telling them their contributions would help "make a pile of money." There was applause. That's when a normally reserved engineer spoke up, "I have to admit that the idea of a big pile of money doesn't do much for me. And the idea of doubling that pile of money does even less." Much to our leader's surprise, that comment received twice the applause. What motivates you might not encourage others. If you want people to feel inspired, you have to offer something that will speak to *them*.

Tips for Inspiration

- Identify and label what your passion feels like.
- Choose specific talking points that speak to people's hearts.
- Be aware that your body language and mood are often mirrored by your followers.
- Give people a common aspiration.
- Come up with a rallying cry.
- Consider your audience; offer a source of encouragement that they will care about.

Summary of Building Alignment

In an aligned organization, every employee—from the executive suite to the loading dock—understands not only the strategy and goals of the business, but also how his or her work contributes to them.
—GEORGE LABOVITZ

Building alignment is the most people-centered part of the VAE model. It's about how you, as a leader, interact with others, how you communicate with and listen to others, and how you and your co-workers affect one another. Each driver of alignment—clarity, dialogue, and inspiration—is about connecting with your team. Clarity leads to understanding. Dialogue facilitates involvement and ownership. Inspiration promotes emotional commitment.

Because building alignment involves the complexity of relationships, being effective requires you to look inside, to do some honest personal reflection on how successfully you interact with others. You may find the skills required to be perfectly natural or you may find it's something you need to stretch toward. A former Danish Navy SEAL who now leads an international consulting firm confided to us how his prior experience in the military didn't quite prepare him for the alignment-building he would need to do in the corporate culture. He remembers, "As a commanding officer, when you say something, that's the truth. No one disputes it. When I began working in the private sector, I expected the same. But when I would say to my team, 'Please do this or do that,' they would look at me and say, 'Why?' I realized I needed to provide a rationale. In my old world, I *was* the rationale!"

As you prepare to do this important interpersonal work, use these tips and reminders to guide your process.

1. Know your audience(s). The answer to the question: "Who do I need to build alignment with?" may seem obvious, especially if you're operating at an executive level of leadership: you want *everyone* aligned. And if you're leading at a team level, you may think you simply need to focus on the members of your immediate workgroup, those for whom you are responsible. But remember that alignment happens at all levels and in multiple directions: top-down, bottom-up, and laterally. Executive leaders explain their rationale to an entire workforce; they must also inspire and exchange perspectives with their executive colleagues. Workgroup leaders encourage and inspire their teams; they must also deliver clear messages to senior leaders about how they're contributing to the larger vision. Make a list of the individuals and groups with whom you must build alignment and note how these multiple audiences may require different levels of clarity, dialogue, and inspiration. Here are some questions to consider:

- **For clarity:** What do they know, need to know, or want to know?
- **For dialogue:** What questions or concerns might they have about the vision?
- **For inspiration:** What motivates them?

The more clearly you can identify and anticipate each of your audiences, the more effectively you can build alignment.

2. Practice the skills. The most effective leaders know that the skills involved in alignment require practice. If you're not in the habit of actively building alignment or if any aspects of this area feel particularly challenging, consider how and where you might practice these essential skills. Choose colleagues or team members with whom you feel comfortable and make them your sounding boards. Try presenting your vision and explaining your rationale to them. Encourage them to provide candid feedback on your communication style or listening skills. Ask them what they find inspirational or what successes they've had inspiring others. Sure, this kind of preparation and rehearsal takes time and effort. But the best leaders will tell you: when it comes to building alignment, practice makes perfect.

3. Continuously build alignment. Remember that building alignment is a dynamic, ongoing process, one that most successful leaders tell us is on their minds *almost* *constantly.* It is not a fixed, one-time event allowing you to "align it and forget it." In fact, alignment happens in various ways throughout the VAE process. The earliest steps toward alignment happen when you're testing assumptions for the vision. Later, the realities of execution can cause the team to stray from the original vision, and you'll need to return to the clear goals and encourage more dialogue to get people back on track. Because it's so people-focused, alignment may require you to adapt to changing needs and circumstances. And while alignment occurs at the macro level, as when an entire organization aligns with a new corporate vision, it also happens in small, day-to-day interactions.

We talked to a vice president of R&D at a training products company who describes just this sort of ongoing alignment: "I got back from a meeting and there were some really important implications for IT in what we discussed. So I walked into our CTO's office and said, 'Do you have a minute?' He said, 'I'm leaving for the airport in five minutes.' So we took those five minutes and I brought him up to speed. Because I knew things I didn't know three days ago, and they were important things. By the time the conversation was over, he said to me, 'We're going in the same direction.'" Clearly, alignment can look different for everyone, but the most important point is that it keeps happening.

Doing the Work: Building Alignment

Know Your Audience(s)

- Who do I need to build alignment with?
- What are your different audience needs?

Summary of Building Alignment

- *For Clarity:* What do they know, need to know, or want to know?
- *For Dialogue:* What questions might they have in mind about the vision?
- *For Inspiration:* What motivates them?

Practice the Skills

- What aspects of building alignment will require the most work?
- Who can be your sounding board?
- Where and when can you practice being clear, encouraging dialogue, inspiring others?

Tips for Clarity

- Be straightforward and transparent.
- Look at it from the listeners' point of view—it needs to make sense to them.
- Monitor people's reactions for comprehension.
- Find the "headline" of your message—you should be able to boil it down to eight words or fewer.
- Create talking points that balance the big picture and the details.
- Refer back to your message repeatedly over time.

Tips for Dialogue

- Create an open and relaxed environment.
- Have one-on-one conversations with people.
- Practice reflective listening.
- Make sure your tone of voice and body language come across as receptive.
- Be careful not to debate or battle for your own side.
- Look for signs of people just telling you what you want to hear; then encourage more honest feedback.

Tips for Inspiration

- Identify and label what your passion feels like.
- Choose specific talking points that speak to people's hearts.
- Be aware that your body language and mood are often mirrored by your followers.
- Give people a common aspiration.
- Come up with a rallying cry.
- Consider your audience; offer a source of encouragement that they will care about.

PART 3

Execution

12

Vision

Alignment

Execution
Momentum
Structure
Feedback

Introduction to Championing Execution

Vision without execution is hallucination.
—Thomas Edison

Once the vision is crafted and people are aligned, how do you as the leader contribute to a successful execution? Research from Teresa Amabile of the Harvard Business School begins to point toward an answer. Amabile studied the social and psychological components necessary for people to produce good work. Of the four components she identified, two deal specifically with a sense of achievement. First, people are most creative and productive when they have a passion for a task that's interesting, involving, personally challenging, or satisfying. Second—and here's where your leadership comes in—cultural and environmental factors stimulate creativity and productivity, such as when leaders encourage a sense of positive challenge in the work, collaboration, and the development of new ideas; and when they support innovation, give appropriate recognition, and create ways to actively share ideas across the organization. In other words, you can create an environment that leads to more effective execution. As the leader, you can instill a sense of the possible in an organization or team, and a personal and tangible feeling that each contribution is a step toward realizing a vision.

What Exactly Do We Mean by Execution?

At its most basic level, execution is *making the vision a reality*. And not just any reality, but the *right* reality, one that takes the imagined future and turns it into a real accomplishment. Execution is how organizations and teams take all the good ideas and turn them into results. Without execution:

- Wal-Mart would never have turned to the distribution process called "cross-docking" to realize Sam Walton's dream of delivering low-priced goods to small towns.
- Corning would never have been able to produce huge quantities of Gorilla Glass that had never been manufactured before to support Steve Jobs' vision for the first iPhone.
- SpaceX would never have been able to become the first privately held company to successfully send cargo to the International Space Station with their Dragon spacecraft.

While leaders may or may not be directly involved in day-to-day implementation and production, they are *always* responsible for ensuring that people have what they need to do their work effectively. This is where your work as a leader requires that you step into a new and critical role: that of champion. *Successful execution of a vision can't happen without the deep commitment and active championing of leaders.*

The Importance of Championing Execution

"To champion" means "to support the cause of someone or something." But what other connotations can help us develop a better understanding of this important leadership role? A champion is

- A *defender* of the time a team needs to work through solutions
- A *proponent* of a better structure or plan to help people achieve
- An *advocate* for the work and workers, praising and offering feedback
- A *lobbyist* for adequate resources and ongoing support
- A *booster* who provides the necessary momentum, drive, or resources

Can a vision be realized without a champion? Sure. Those responsible for carrying out the work may still finish the job—if the vision is clear enough and alignment is strong enough. But will the result of their efforts lead to the vision as imagined? And more important to the organization's continued success, will the *next* vision be realized if the leader is perceived as disinterested and unsupportive? Championing execution is as much about establishing and defining your credibility as an effective leader as it is about helping the organization or team achieve the vision. Even dedicated, independent, and highly competent teams require deliberate and committed leadership.

Leaders who are deeply committed and actively engaged understand that execution is a process, not an endpoint. They know their involvement is absolutely essential for three key reasons:

1. Championing execution is a tangible sign of the leader's commitment. Thomas Edison famously said that "genius is 1 percent inspiration and 99 percent perspiration," which is a good indicator of the brand of dauntless determination he promoted. In his quest to produce a commercially viable light bulb with a long-burning filament, he drove his team to test no fewer than 6,000 materials. Similarly, leaders who champion execution persevere, sticking around to ensure the promise is fulfilled, rather than moving on to the next best thing. They make certain people have the resources they need to persist and the environment that allows them to stay focused. Support and advocacy from a leader confirms the vision is not just talk, not just aspiration, and is something that can really be done, something that is within reach.

2. Championing execution assures the development of concrete strategies. No matter how strongly people align with a vision, they will ask, "How are we going to get there?" In the top-down view of execution, leaders may communicate the strategy only as an aspirational goal. But when a leader champions execution, he makes sure that a priority is placed on developing strategies and is fully present in the process.

3. Championing execution gives people a sense of achievement. As Amabile's research shows, a sense of achievement is critical to people doing their best work. Without a champion to create an environment that supports this sense of achievement, people may still complete tasks, but they may become disengaged, resentful, or lack any fulfillment beyond collecting a paycheck. As the president of a company who inherited an organization with a poor record of execution told us, "One of the first things I had to do was have everyone stop looking at me as the person who pays them. Our customers are the ones who pay us, and when we realize that, we remember our purpose and redefine our achievements."

Execution at All Levels

Execution is, perhaps, the most obvious step in a company's process: if you don't execute, you are lost. In spite of this, it is often the most overlooked aspect for leaders in the VAE model. Like vision and alignment, execution happens at all levels, not just at the foot of the mountain. The role of all leaders, at all levels, is to make sure the strategies, people, and culture are in place for the vision to become reality. However, certain aspects of this leadership role may look different depending on where you are in the organization.

- You may be more or less hands-on.
- Your primary role may be to advocate for resources or to provide them.
- You may create strategy or you may ensure strategies are followed.
- You may establish the culture or you may support it.

At whatever level you lead, you are still championing execution, creating the environment that allows everyone to work successfully toward realizing the vision.

In the VAE model, championing execution depends on three drivers, which you'll read about in the next chapters: Momentum, Structure, and Feedback. Let's start by taking a look at the importance of a sense of momentum.

13

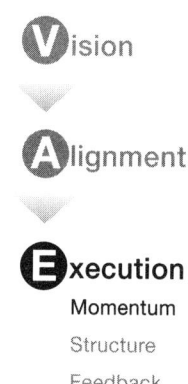

Championing Execution Through Momentum

The speed of the leader determines the pace of the pack.
—Ralph Waldo Emerson

If you were lucky as a kid, someone in your neighborhood had a pool. And even though the in-ground ones were usually the first choice, there was one advantage to those circular above-ground pools—you could make a whirlpool. When all the kids walked in the same direction for about five minutes (especially the big kids), you'd have a really strong current. After that, it took on a life of its own. Try and swim against it. Then swim as fast as you can with it. It's fun. That's what it's like working in an organization with momentum—it's still work, but it's fun.

Of all the drivers in the VAE model, momentum is perhaps the most intuitive. Anyone who watches sporting events or has ever been on a successful team knows what it feels like. When things start going well, you just seem to get all the breaks. So who wouldn't want to have momentum on his side?

Indeed, the case for momentum is well documented. For decades leadership gurus have touted it in one form or another. Since Tom Peters popularized the idea of a "bias for action" in his 1980s blockbuster *In Search of Excellence*, it's become a well-recognized core principle of successful organizations. Perennial best-selling author John Maxwell calls momentum "a leader's best friend," with one of its virtues being the ability to accentuate the positive, making success seem more certain and challenges more manageable. With momentum, the focus isn't on the pain of what people are doing, but on the satisfaction that the eventual outcome will bring. Maxwell also reminds us that it's harder to *create* momentum than to keep it going. This observation is probably familiar to most of us. If there is one thing we can relate to from high school physics class, it's Newton's first law, commonly called the "Law of Inertia." This is the idea that a body at rest tends to remain at rest, and a body in motion tends to stay in motion. You might also remember that the larger the "body" (or group, in the case of an organization), the more energy it takes to start it moving. Fortunately, physics also dictates that, once they do start moving, larger objects are harder to stop as well. So it might be a challenge to get things rolling, particularly for large organizations. But once you're on the good side of inertia, it generally feels like the wind is at your back.

The other commonly noted need for momentum occurs during times of organizational change. John Kotter, the renowned expert on leadership and change, amassed more than thirty years of research showing that 70 percent of major change efforts in organizations fail. Remarkably, more than 50 percent of those failures occur at the first step in Kotter's Eight-Step Process for Leading Change, "Establishing a Sense of Urgency." In times of change, complacency is not easily overcome. And Kotter reminds us that, to create a lasting sense of urgency, leaders need to appeal to both the head and the heart.

Peters, Maxwell, and Kotter all sing the praises of momentum, albeit with somewhat different language and emphasis. But one thing they clearly agree on is that momentum is the leader's responsibility. It is the leader who makes sure that a passion for achieving the vision is transferred to the rest of the group. And while there are skills involved, momentum actually starts with the mindset of the leader, who consciously chooses the pace and recognizes that creating a sense of urgency is vital.

The leader has to make the call about what's reasonable in setting goals—putting a stake in the ground for what the group is going to accomplish and making sure the goals are challenging enough without being impossible. Momentum isn't rushing for the sake of rushing. It is fluid, ongoing motion—the shared drive to do things sooner rather than later. Momentum comes from a mentality that the work we do contributes directly to our success and that we are eager to accomplish our goals every step of the way.

At the same time, leaders have to remember that momentum is about carrying the team forward in an agreed-on direction—toward the vision. We need to be conscious about keeping that forward motion, and when the vision evolves, we have to keep people aligned.

Experienced leaders know that they cannot build and maintain momentum alone. Leaders at all levels must see initiating momentum as their responsibility and work to establish a culture of momentum. They see to it that this mindset is transferred to everyone on their teams. How does this transfer happen? In this chapter, we'll break down how skilled leaders set and communicate high expectations for momentum through the two drivers of momentum in the VAE model—*being driven* and *initiating action*.

Execution
Momentum
▶ Being Driven

It was the first morning of the annual ASTD (American Society for Training and Development) conference before the opening keynote. In the convention center lobby, we ran into Jan, one of the most successful consultants we work with. Most people were chatting, drinking skim lattes, and waiting for the giant expo hall to open. Jan was refining a two-page list of the things she was going to get out of the conference—that day. "Wow, that's an amazing list. You are ambitious," we commented. "I grew up poor," she responded. "I never waste an opportunity." Never wasting an opportunity—that's driven.

In a nutshell, drive is pushing yourself and others forward. People who are driven believe things could always be better, and they're eager to prove it. There's an impatience about them—but in a good way. We know a boss with a sign outside his office that reads, "Impatience is a virtue." You pick up on that pretty quickly. Everyone knows that we never waste an opportunity. At the extreme, this can lead to burnout or resentment, but when it's done right, it makes work more engaging. It creates that current that you want to swim in, and you feel like you're a part of something that's alive and dynamic.

Driven leaders aren't just personally ambitious; their ambition is infectious. In fact, it may be more apt to call it "driving." They send the message that they want to keep things moving, and they're willing to press people, to say, "Come on guys, we need to pick up the pace."

But pushing people can be uncomfortable and can create tension that many of us would prefer not to deal with. This can be particularly tough for those who are more low-key—the classic Type B personality. These leaders may have high standards, but they don't always communicate that. The message is more often, "Hey, just do your best. You'll get it done when you get it done. That's cool." The result? You may end up with a few go-getters on the team, but for the most part people settle into complacency. They set their sights on comfortable—and usually achieve it.

This can also be more of a problem for novice leaders. In fact, our research shows that inexperienced leaders may find it more difficult to drive people to push themselves harder. Experienced leaders not only know this is part of their jobs, but they've grown much more comfortable playing this role in the group.

New leaders need to remind themselves that people genuinely want a leader with high standards. Our research shows that there is a positive correlation between being a leader who sets high expectations and being a leader people say they like working with, and between setting high expectations and being respected as a leader in the organization, as indicated in Table 13.1.

Table 13.1. Ratings of Leaders Who Set High or Low Expectations

	Among leaders who set high expectations	Among leaders who set low expectations
Percentage of people who said . . .		
He/she is a good leader.	86	12
He/she is respected as a good leader in the organization.	82	13
I enjoy working with him/her.	91	42

Leaders recognize that people tend to live up or down to whatever expectations are set about how quickly things can be accomplished. Then how do we become driving leaders without becoming tyrants? How do you, as the leader, gain the confidence to push people to be the best versions of themselves?

Strategies for Being Driven

A fast-paced organization doesn't have to be a stressed-out organization—being driven can actually increase both productivity and satisfaction.

First, as Jim Kouzes and Barry Posner describe in their classic best-seller, *The Leadership Challenge*, remember to "Model the Way." In other words, never ask your people to work any harder than you are working or to maintain a level of sustained energy that you aren't committed to yourself. As the authors remind us, "No one will believe you're serious until they see you doing what you're asking of others. Leading by example is how leaders make visions and values tangible." While practicing what you preach is always the right thing to do, it's really not optional in driving momentum. It's unrealistic to expect that followers will move faster or push harder than their leaders do.

Next, commit your team to deadlines related to external events, for example, a major conference or the end of the fiscal year. An external commitment is always harder to break—someone else is waiting, counting on you. A lot of us like to have a cushion. We hedge our bets and create some wiggle room on our timelines. Of course, it's only prudent to expect unforeseeable delays and obstacles, but an appropriately tight outside commitment creates a bit of tension. It's useful tension, however, and it's shared by most highly successful teams. The fear of failure blends with the passion to win, creating strong momentum.

Finally, be aware of how much time you take between meetings on a project. Here's a typical scenario: The group meets and identifies some next steps. Toward the end, someone says, "Okay, let's meet next week to keep this moving." Maybe there's a good reason to wait until next week, but usually this is just the expected pace—we wait a few days between meetings and decisions. But let's do some simple math. If a decision or project is going to take five meetings and we wait a week between meetings, that's five weeks. If we have those meetings every day, that's one week. We just saved four weeks. Now we know that all of us have a lot on our plates, but as the leader, you are in a position to say, "Wait, why can't we pick this up tomorrow, or better yet, later today?" It may take a while, but eventually this pace trickles down to others. There's an unspoken assumption that we don't wait around.

xecution
Momentum
▶ Initiating Action

As most of us have experienced, certain people seem to have a passion for dwelling on what is wrong with the system. They sigh with exasperation at the people who make the rules—the people who are so out-of-touch. At the end of the day, however, people with this mentality are resigned to trudge along in their broken, unjust worlds. They're victims of the incompetent, ignorant people with real power.

Okay, now contrast that picture with the following. Another group of people sees an inefficiency or a way that their jobs could be done better, and they assume the responsibility to make the change happen. They're not Pollyannas. They can clearly picture the obstacles and resistance they'll have to wade through. Their assumption, however, is that (1) it is their duty to see these changes through and (2) with enough effort, they will make it happen. It is a deep-seated mindset. They see themselves as empowered to change their worlds.

What's the difference between the first scenario and the second? The people in the second are leaders, and those in the first are not. The essence of what we are talking about here is initiative—taking responsibility for change when you have the option to look the other way or kick it down the road. It is the assumption that you will make it happen, and not some other mystery person in some other department at some other time.

The leader pushes down that first domino—acts rather than reacts. This means jumping on opportunities when they present themselves instead of just passively waiting for the directives to trickle down. Even when executing, when the vision is in place, you still need some of that entrepreneurial spirit, someone who is identifying and seizing opportunities to do things better. For example, let's say that in the middle of executing on your vision, there's a reorganization in your department. Upper management has thought through the big issues and you certainly have the option to simply go with the flow. But as the leader, you spot an opportunity to build a partnership with IT that was never possible before. Changes to corporate policy mean that you have access to a wider range of vendors. You recognize a small window to advocate for getting rid of red tape that has held your team back for years. This is initiating above and beyond the original plan.

Still, this doesn't come naturally to all of us. Initiating requires outward energy on a regular basis, and that can be pretty tough. However, as leaders, we must find the energy to champion new initiatives and model a stance that says we're not only open to ideas for improvement, but we thrive on them. At a minimum, this is about initiating around difficulties that arise during execution. It's taking the initiative to pursue the next step or to explore what seemed a little off in the last step. And it's doing this proactively, before what seemed "a little off" becomes a major derailment. Let's take a look at a few ways you can make initiating action a bigger part of your leadership repertoire.

Strategies for Initiating Action

There's one factor above all others that keeps leaders from taking on more initiatives: they're already busy. If they have unscheduled time during the month, it's likely to be swallowed up putting out fires or dealing with unforeseen complications. If new initiatives are going to make it onto your plate, you need to challenge your priorities. You need to step back and say, "What are the most important things we could be doing to make a difference right now?" As a leader, you need to see this as part of your job, as important as any other part.

If initiating doesn't come naturally to you, work to develop a habit of focusing on the most important challenges or goals your team faces. It doesn't take much time, but it does require a conscious effort. Find a specific time to check in with yourself every morning before you arrive at work. Make it part of your routine, perhaps before you climb out of bed, while you're brushing your teeth, or as you walk the dog around the block. Ask yourself a simple question like, "If we only have time for one thing that's not on the schedule, what's the single most important thing we can do today to reach our goals?" Don't be discouraged if you don't accomplish these daily goals. Be patient and keep at it every day. It's a great way to remind yourself of your responsibility as a leader to push your team forward.

Finally, start to redefine "above and beyond" as the new normal. Recognize, and perhaps even over-recognize, instances when people are proactive. This is where we come back to expectations. Help people see taking on new initiatives as part of their jobs. Perhaps go so far as writing it into their quarterly or yearly objectives. And most important, if someone has an idea for a change, take it seriously. Genuinely listen and make sure he knows that his resourcefulness and gumption are not only appreciated, but seen as crucial to the group's success.

Tips for Momentum

- Lead by example—never ask people for more momentum than you are willing to take on yourself.
- Commit your team to deadlines related to external events.
- Reduce the time between meetings on projects.
- Challenge your priorities to make time for initiating action.
- Focus on choosing the single most important new initiative every day.
- Recognize proactivity and help people see new initiatives as part of their jobs.

14

Vision

Alignment

Execution
Momentum
Structure
Feedback

Championing Execution Through Structure

By failing to prepare, you are preparing to fail.
—Benjamin Franklin

Providing structure is a big task. It's tangible, it's complex, and it's time-consuming. It's also the point where we encountered the most pushback when we were developing the VAE model. Because when it comes to the tasks that are required to provide structure, we often heard, "That's not leadership—that's management." It became clear that if there's one aphorism consultants have relied on to explain the difference between management and leadership, it is, "Managers manage tasks and leaders lead people."

We traced the roots of this thinking all the way back to 1900 when Henri Fayol, the managing director of a French mining company, delivered a speech at the International Mining Congress in Paris. In that address, Fayol encouraged the audience to begin giving "the administrative function" as much attention as the technical aspects of running their companies. At the time they did not realize they were witnessing the dawn of a new era of management theory.

By 1916, Fayol's work in the new field of business administration was published and identified the five functions of management as:

1. Planning
2. Organizing
3. Commanding (or Directing)
4. Coordinating, and
5. Controlling

Now that management had been well-defined as task-oriented, people sought to differentiate leadership as people-oriented. Over the course of the following century, recognized thought leaders Peter Drucker, Warren Bennis, and others wrote extensively (some might even say excessively) on the distinctions between management and leadership. Today, a quick Google search on the difference between management and leadership retrieves about twenty million hits.

If so many people see tasks as a manager's role rather than a leader's, why did we include the task of providing structure in our leadership model? Ultimately, we were persuaded by the best-selling 2002 book *Execution: The*

Discipline of Getting Things Done by former chairman and CEO of Honeywell International Larry Bossidy and world-renowned management consultant Ram Charan. In it, they challenge the belief that the execution of the vision is to be left to managers and is somehow beneath or separate from the work of leaders.

The authors go on to detail common excuses for avoiding responsibility for execution, such as the importance of delegating and empowering, or the risk of being seen as micromanagers. But Bossidy and Charan are relentless in their determination to dispel the misconception that leaders are supposed to be visionaries who conceive brilliant ideas and insights and then leave it to the managers to accomplish the job.

While the Bossidy and Charan book is easily the most comprehensive and convincing work we studied in this area, they are not alone in their opinions. Former Baxter International CEO Harry Kraemer is just as vehement about leaders rolling up their sleeves and staying close to the action. In his experience, ". . . execution and implementation go awry for a number of reasons that have more to do with the individual leader than with the organization or any outside influence. . . . In these cases, the leader doesn't want to get that close to the ground level where things happen." He also questions the false distinction between leaders and managers, suggesting that they're not mutually exclusive, and concludes that you can't be a good leader without being a good manager.

So which execution tasks have we included within the work of leaders? Our conversation has come full circle back to "planning," the very first item on Henri Fayol's 1916 list of the five functions of management. But now, nearly one hundred years later, we include *providing a plan* that brings together people, strategy, and operations as part of our VAE leadership model.

xecution
Structure
▶ Providing a Plan

It's an annual challenge for our small team: create a lab environment for our best customers that will engage them, deliver the latest product information, share best practices, and give these hundreds of consultants from around the world an opportunity to network and learn from each other. And we deliver it all over a period of just forty-eight hours so attendees can limit the time they spend away from their clients.

We refine the vision and make sure everyone on the team is aligned. Now we face the exhausting challenge of pulling it off. For it to work, everyone needs to know and do a part, and everything must fit together. Such an event requires content, presenters, timelines, budgeting, logistics, marketing, and so many other details and resources.

What we need at this point is structure, a framework to pull it all together, a plan. We follow the old adage, "begin with the end in mind" and start with The Program—a blueprint that forces us to think about the people, strategies, and operations needed to flawlessly execute our bold vision.

The Program spells it all out—the details of who, what, when, where, why, and how. It even covers the realm of if. We anticipate problems so that solutions are waiting in the wings. When unexpected problems do arise during the event, everyone on the team understands the overall goal and knows what his or her role is. People are able to make quick decisions to resolve the issues and keep the event running smoothly. And this structure extends beyond the team to the attendees, who all receive a clearly communicated agenda and know what to expect. Ultimately, the event receives high marks from our customers, and it's a triumph for our small but mighty team.

Earlier in this book, we said that diving into the details should be put on hold when crafting a vision. But those details can't be kept on hold forever. By focusing on the planning process, the leader assures there is time to bring them to the forefront and to give these details deliberate attention. Providing a plan for moving from Point A to Point B not only assures that the right people will be doing the right things at the right time, but it also allows those people to know when they will be needed and when they will be free to contribute to other activities outside the project. A plan ensures that everyone is on the same page and provides a common foundation for the team to refer back to and rely on.

So does this mean that, as a leader, you have to draw up the plan and understand every detail? The best answer is "it depends," but in most cases the answer is "no." Your contribution to creating the plan and the level of detail the plan requires are dependent on your leadership role, as well as on the experience of your team and the type of work they are undertaking. If you're a front-line leader in a small, entrepreneurial organization, you may be very immersed in the details, while a CEO at a large organization may be more concerned with convincing the leaders who report to him to invest in planning. Small teams working in customary roles on familiar projects typically need a less detailed plan than very large teams working on highly complex projects do.

However, every leader is still responsible for making sure the right level of planning happens. Regardless of who takes on the brunt of the work of creating the plan or the level of detail that it contains, what's important is that the plan provide a sufficient structure for the work at hand. Leaders need to understand the value such structure brings and set aside the time required to create robust and realistic plans.

Strategies for Providing a Plan

One of the most effective ways to gain a team's buy-in is to involve them in the planning process. Not only does this increase their support for the work they'll be doing, but it also increases the reliability of the plan itself. After all, who knows better what's involved in a task than the person who will be doing the work? If the activities being planned are unfamiliar to the team, it's important to find people who *have* been there and done that. They can offer insight into the amount of work involved, how long it might take, and what it might cost—and even point out what could go wrong.

Next, as you begin to map out the plan, encourage everyone involved to ask this question about each step: "If we are successful doing this, will it materially help to close the gap between where we are and where we are trying to go?" By consistently applying this discipline, you will be able to keep plans robust and sharply focused.

Finally, remember that planning is an iterative process. Those high-level requirements you start with may very well change as the team explores the details of how things will unfold. More often than not, changes to one part of the plan will affect other parts. Creating a realistic plan can be complicated and messy, and it takes time. As a leader, it's important to stay plugged in to the planning process so you can provide the resources and time needed to allow this messiness to be worked out. Doing so increases the likelihood that the team will produce consistent—and desired—results.

xecution
Structure
▶ Analyzing In-Depth

There are few creatures in the animal kingdom that can plan like Wile E. Coyote. Here we have a guy who's not afraid to strap dynamite to a boomerang or pour nitroglycerin into hollowed-out carrots. These are some highly elaborate schemes. And yet, he's had exactly zero success in his obsession with the Road Runner. Why? Well, part of it might be poor depth perception, and part of it may be that he is perhaps a bit of a sociopath. But more fundamentally, his plans lack rigor. He's failed to understand all of the variables he will inevitably encounter (for example, boomerangs are designed to return to their owners). And perhaps just as important, he hasn't considered all of the variables that he might encounter (such as oncoming hang glider traffic). Further, he's failed to examine his plans in light of his core assumptions and basic goals. (Is there a way to get food that doesn't involve a hypersonic bird?) His failure isn't due to lack of planning, it's due to a lack of in-depth planning.

Analyzing in-depth is really about appreciating the true purpose of the execution and having a firm handle on all the moving parts. Understanding the connections makes it easier to anticipate what will work and what won't. It also helps pinpoint where there might be an opportunity for a shortcut or when something could be cut out altogether.

The complex, iterative planning process we've described can't be accomplished without critical thinking. To build a solid, reliable structure, doing an in-depth analysis of the execution challenges is essential. And the bigger the project, the more difficult it is to anticipate all of the contingencies.

Furthermore, this need for in-depth analysis doesn't disappear once a plan is in place and the work is underway. The ability to anticipate the cause-and-effect mechanisms that play out during execution is a key part of successfully executing a plan. It involves doing research when issues arise. It means looking at the root causes of problems and finding the essence of what has gone wrong—and what has gone right, for that matter.

So how much of the critical thinking and in-depth analysis is up to you as the leader? As with planning, your level of involvement will vary based on your particular leadership role, on your team's experience, and on the type of work being done. While you don't need to understand every detail, you must have a strong sense of what's involved. It's also important to encourage other people on the team to think critically about the execution of the plans.

Strategies for Analyzing In-Depth

For those of us who would rather make a quick decision and move on, in-depth analysis can be painful. But that's nothing compared to the pain we are likely to feel later if we ignore it. The good news is that the leader doesn't have to go it alone. Leaders can—and should—involve the team.

First, create an environment in which there is consistent and timely communication across functions. Everyone should know where she is in the process and understand how what she does affects other parts. Having a comprehensive plan in place certainly helps, but we all know that things don't always go according to plan. That's when it helps to have a shared understanding of how the pieces are connected. If a change is required or there's a problem, people must know what else could be affected, rather than thinking exclusively about their own domains.

Next, challenge yourself and your team to think critically about what *might* happen on the project, as well as the root causes of people, strategy, and operations issues that do arise. Think of risks—things that could go wrong—and either eliminate them or plan what to do if they occur. Remember the project "PreMortem" from Chapter 5? This may be the time to revisit the potential implications that were surfaced at that time. But don't just focus on the negative; dedicate some time to thinking about what could go right. Are there any new opportunities that might arise as a result of the work being done or the relationships being built on the project? Is there anything the team can do to enhance these opportunities?

Finally, be deliberate about allowing plenty of time for planning and analysis. Of course, for every vision, there is an end date in mind, a goal. But leaving time to build an effective structure—to create a realistic plan and do the appropriate analysis—will ultimately increase the likelihood of achieving that goal and will make the path to it much smoother.

Tips for Structure

- Involve the people who will actually be doing the work in the planning process.
- Ensure that plans are robust and sharply focused.
- Expect planning to be an iterative process.
- Create an environment in which there is consistent and timely communication across functions.
- Think critically about what might happen and what has happened.
- Allow time for planning and doing the appropriate analysis.

15

Championing Execution Through Feedback

The single biggest problem in communication is the illusion that it has taken place.
—George Bernard Shaw

Think back to the last time you were learning a new card game. You may have had a teacher who had the players put their cards on the table face up, so he could explain what's going on. He could describe what strategy to use, given your hand. He could point out when you were making a mistake. He could compliment you when you did it right. It wasn't enough for him to simply explain the rules—he wanted to give you continuous feedback. And he could only give you such clear feedback because everyone's cards were on the table. There was complete transparency.

Perhaps after a few rounds you decided that you were ready for the big leagues. People shook their heads at your hubris and picked up their cards. The transparency disappeared. And what happened to the feedback from your teacher? It dropped off a cliff. Most of the learning from that point on was what you could figure out for yourself.

Of course, in a card game it makes sense to pick up your cards. You're competing. You don't want other people to know what you're planning to do. On a team, it's the exact opposite (or at least, it *should* be the exact opposite). Figuratively speaking, everyone's playing a hand. With our cards face up on the table, we can communicate clearly. We can point out when projects are off track. We can quickly recognize and spread someone's brilliant innovation. As a leader, one of your most important roles in execution is to build a culture with this kind of transparency and feedback. You need to persuade people to put their cards face up on the table.

Feedback requires you as the leader to *be involved*. You must get your hands dirty and really understand what's going on in the trenches. It's critical to see everyone's hand. Even though this may sound like a no-brainer, leaders, particularly those at the top, often fail to keep their fingers on the pulse of their organizations. Too often, information is filtered and summarized so extensively before it reaches the leader that it becomes almost impossible to develop any meaningful insights that can lead to productive feedback.

In fact, delivering feedback does not appear to be the norm, and it's a discipline that many leaders at all levels seem to regard as discretionary. Take, for instance, a study by The Ken Blanchard Companies. They surveyed 1,400 leaders, managers, and executives, asking them: "What are the top five things that leaders most often fail to do when working with others?" The number one answer was: "Failing to provide appropriate feedback (praise, redirection)." This ranked above even important topics like listening and setting clear goals.

The VAE model looks at two aspects of feedback: *addressing problems* and *offering praise.* When we asked leaders to rate how well they do with each of these practices, we made some interesting discoveries (see Table 15.1). First, leaders are more than twice as likely to see themselves as very good at "giving praise" as they are at "addressing problems." Furthermore, in our analysis, fewer than one in twelve leaders claims to excel at both feedback practices.

While either addressing problems or giving praise may come naturally to you, it's unlikely that both of them do. And, since it seems to be the most difficult for leaders to do really well, let's start by taking a look at addressing problems.

Table 15.1. Leaders' Self-Ratings on Giving Praise and Addressing Problems

Excelled at . . .	Percent
Giving praise	56
Addressing problems	24
Both giving praise and addressing problems	7

xecution
Feedback
▶ Addressing Problems

Imagine you're an artist. You spend an entire day toiling away, pouring your heart and soul into your creation. The next morning you bring your work to the table and an entire team of people rip it apart. They pick at everything you've done. Then you go back to your desk and do the whole thing again and the cycle repeats.

Welcome to Pixar, where some of the world's best-loved animated films of all time have been created—in exactly this way. It's something they refer to as "crit" sessions (critic sessions), and they swear by them. Every day, artists subject their work to rigorous evaluation. It doesn't always feel fantastic, but they wouldn't give it up. This process of sharing and evaluating each other's ideas is the norm, and everyone knows that it's one of the most important ingredients in their success.

What Pixar has done is to create a culture where candor is the norm. People speak up about problems, and it's no big deal. Having this sort of culture, however, is a big deal. It's also rare. We asked a sample of workers: "In your organization, how often are problems that need attention addressed in an open and straightforward manner?" Only 31 percent said that this happens regularly. Most of us have worked in places where inefficiencies linger and poor performance is accepted as "satisfactory." These teams and organizations are never going to be anything more than passable, and yet this knowledge doesn't seem to be enough for leaders to speak up about problems. So we decided to investigate just why it's so hard for leaders to be candid.

As Table 15.2 shows, the number one reason for not speaking up is "political factors." It's a broad term, but most of us know what it means. It's that entanglement of alliances, self-serving agendas, grudges, prejudices, legacies, and personal insecurities that is so infuriating to people who really want to make a difference.

If you have a highly political culture, it's probably its own brand of mess. It would be naïve of us to try to explain how to navigate your jungle. What we will say, however, is that, to be a truly effective leader, you cannot resign yourself to keep quiet about problems because of that culture. You'll need to show tough-minded fortitude.

Now "tough-minded fortitude" may not be your thing. That's okay. But what you need to remember is that being a

Table 15.2. What Keeps You from Speaking Up About Problems More Often?

Feedback	Percent
Political factors	50.3
I don't want to stir up tension.	32.2
I have a fairly non-confrontational personality.	28.2
I don't want to hurt people's feelings.	17.4
I don't want to discourage people.	17.4
It wouldn't actually improve things around here.	11.4
It means that I would have to spend more of my time fixing problems.	7.4
It's not my job.	4

leader means occasionally inviting stress into your world when you have the option of not issuing that invitation. There's a reason that half as many leaders say they excel at "addressing problems" as "giving praise." Addressing problems is tough. It means disrupting the harmony. When you look at the other top reasons leaders give for not speaking up, many are tied to a desire to maintain harmony. We want to avoid confrontations and hurt feelings. We don't want to interrupt the flow of progress. It's easy to understand the temptation to smooth it all over.

Furthermore, many prominent role models for being candid are negative. In fact, some people actually do enjoy criticizing and calling others out. School kids have a name for this: bullying. And to be sure, if candor is done recklessly, it kills transparency. Who is going to want to leave her cards face up if it's going to result in being berated?

But if done with respect, addressing problems in a straightforward manner actually enhances transparency. As at Pixar, direct feedback can become the norm. People understand that they're going to screw up occasionally, and that's okay. Everyone accepts that problems are a part of life. As the leader, you don't blame people or point fingers, but you also don't sweep problems under the rug—you surface them so they can be solved. By modeling the right way to point out problems and give corrective feedback, you can create a more open, productive culture on your team.

Strategies for Addressing Problems

Because the goal is a culture of candor, transparency, and trust, you can start by making yourself vulnerable. Acknowledge decisions that were less than fantastic. Keep people accountable, but err on the side of over-faulting yourself for bad calls. You're the role model who demonstrates *there is nobility to acknowledging my mistakes and growing from them.*

Next, have regular, semi-formal dialogues about what isn't working. This is the opposite of an anonymous suggestion box. People need to hear the message that there's nothing to fear in calling out problems. A few months ago, we interviewed Dan, an R&D director of an international pharmaceutical company. Here's how he, as the leader, convinces people to lay their cards on the table, face up.

> *"I meet with between ten and twelve individuals who are more or less randomly put together. So it's not just one department, but it's different departments. And I kick the managers out. And I just ask people, 'What's going on? What works and what doesn't?' And with that I build a culture over time of people telling me, actually telling me what's going on, because at least the second time around they realize there's no retribution for negative news; quite the opposite, often we can do something about it. And that permeates an organization."*

Finally, focus on the problems and not on the people. Keep everyone's eyes on the prize. The goal is to find a solution, not to place blame. The purpose of exploring what went wrong is to help get it right. In our interviews we found several examples of high-level leaders who would make a point of writing a personal note to people after giving them tough feedback. The notes acknowledged the issue, but they also gave encouragement. In many cases, people held onto the notes for years, using them as a motivation boost. The point is to let people know that the group wants them to succeed and that continued growth is a huge part of success.

Execution
Feedback

▶ Offering Praise

Are people receiving enough praise in the workplace? In our research, we find that, when given the chance, 40 percent of followers ask their leaders to do a better job of acknowledging their contributions. Yet, when we ask leaders how well they do at giving praise, fewer than one in twenty admits "I don't do a very good job." This suggests that there are a lot of leaders out there who are in the dark.

What exactly do people want out of their leaders? Table 15.3 shows the most frequent comments given to leaders regarding the need to offer more praise.

When you read through this list of comments, you can see that one core human need underlies them all—we all need to know that we are valuable. It might feel a little pathetic to say out loud or even admit it to ourselves, but more of our motivations, relationships, and insecurities are driven by this simple psychological need than any other. We want to know that we have worth as people.

When people feel valued by their leader and their group, it becomes a part of them. They internalize the group's goals, and their work has meaning. Conversely, when people don't feel appreciated, they slowly remove themselves from the group emotionally. Why should they care if it succeeds? After all, they're just fulfilling a contract—they put in work and, in return, they receive a paycheck. It's transactional.

Table 15.3. Comments Given to Leaders About Feedback

Comments (from most to least frequent)
He/she doesn't always seem aware of the contributions we make.
I don't always know if he/she's happy with the work I'm doing.
He/she acknowledges some people's contributions more than others.
He/she seems to take people's efforts for granted.
I have no idea whether or not he/she values my work.
He/she seems unaware of his/her employees' contributions.
It seems like he/she only recognizes the same few people.
Actually, he/she gives people credit so often that it sometimes seems insincere.
At times, he/she seems to take too much credit for other people's work.
He/she often seems to take credit for other people's work.
I have to point out my contributions in order to get any acknowledgement from him/her.
Actually, he/she sometimes spends too much time acknowledging contributions.
Actually, he/she sometimes gives people credit that they haven't earned.

So how much do you actually appreciate the people you lead? Sure, you probably like most of them and want the best for them. But do you stop and marvel at their talents? Do you let yourself be absorbed in gratitude for how much work they put in? Basically, how often do you take time to sit back and just appreciate them? If the answer is "not very often," you're not alone. It's not that we're ungrateful, but we just tend to be task-oriented at work. "Marveling" or "being absorbed in gratitude" aren't on the to-do list. In our research, the number one reason leaders say they don't give praise more often is: "It doesn't occur to me in the moment." Someone does a good job and that's great, but the person just moves on to the next step.

At the end of the day, you could simply put "give people more praise" on your to-do list, but there's much greater potential here. The leaders who are able to use praise to genuinely transform their groups actually experience a deep, heartfelt appreciation for the people they lead. When you feel this way, you don't need reminders to give praise. Surprisingly, this may have even more benefits for you than it does for your followers. A variety of studies have found that being appreciative actually increases a person's happiness. When you take deliberate time to appreciate others, you and the people you lead can begin to see work as more than just a series of tasks. The group attitude goes beyond responsibility and accountability—which is good—to purpose and aspiration—which is transformative.

Strategies for Offering Praise

First, based on the data, it's important that you don't assume that people know you appreciate their work. Make a conscious effort to prioritize acknowledging people's contributions. Celebrate milestones and build recognition opportunities into your plans. Be sure to pass along outside praise, too. If someone sends you an email that says the group did a good job, forward it on to everyone involved. At the same time, don't wait for a specific achievement or milestone to express appreciation. Imagine approaching someone, out of the blue, and saying, "Hey, I was just thinking last night about how much work you've been doing on this. Thanks." The fact that it is not tied to a major accomplishment lets the person know that her work is being appreciated all of the time.

Next, make sure your praise is genuine. People can tell when you're truly appreciative of what they've done. Pick out contributions that you know people are proud of and that are really making a difference. Complimenting people is important, but how it happens should be personal and fit the accomplishment. Furthermore, be sure to go beyond the simple "good job." Be specific and paint a picture of the difference the person is making.

Finally, in order to give genuine praise, keep up-to-date. You need to know what people are actually doing, what's going on at the ground level. A compliment has even more meaning when people can see that you've invested the time to really understand what's going on.

Tips for Feedback

- Create a culture of candor and trust by acknowledging your own mistakes.
- Have regular, semi-formal dialogues about what isn't working.
- Focus on the problems and not the people.
- Make a conscious effort to prioritize acknowledging people's contributions.
- Make sure your praise is genuine.
- Keep up-to-date on progress and contributions.

16

Vision

Alignment

Execution
Momentum
Structure
Feedback

Summary of Championing Execution

There are basically two types of people. People who accomplish things, and people who claim to have accomplished things. The first group is less crowded.
—MARK TWAIN

According to a recent study conducted by the authors of *Change Anything*, a book on achieving personal success, 97 percent of surveyed employees report they have some "career-limiting habits" that keep them from achieving their potential at work. Of the career-limiting habits mentioned, the second-most-common one is the routine utterance of these four words: "It's not my job."

This unhelpful workplace attitude is not limited to team members who resist doing a bit more when asked to support the team. When it comes to execution, leaders can be just as guilty of saying, "It's not my job," leaving to others the work of turning vision into reality. But as we've seen, championing execution is a core piece of the VAE model.

As the champion, you are always acting in service of someone or something, whether it is your team, your vision, or your customers. Your energy is focused outward as you seek ways to establish momentum, provide structure, and offer feedback. As a way of starting the work of championing execution, consider the tasks and projects you have around you right now. Think again of the other connotations for the word *champion*. Then ask yourself these questions:

1. Who or what can I *defend*? What vision-critical person, process, or idea could use a protector right about now? What kind of defense might she need in order to complete her role successfully? More time or resources? Protection from interruptions to her work? Some good press around the office? Defending also means fighting for people's right to argue or express dissent by creating an atmosphere of candor and openness; and it may sometimes mean taking the heat so people don't become mired in political battles that pull them off track.

2. For whom can I be a *proponent* or *advocate*? What good work is being done toward making the vision real that is perhaps suffering from skepticism or a lack of attention? UCLA basketball coaching legend John Wooden suggested: "Go out of your way to praise those 'quiet' performers who make things happen. In every organization there are those vital individuals who seem to get things done with little effort and less notice. . . . These are the people who make the trains run on time, and they deserve your attention." Is there a team, colleague, or concept that could use a cheerleader? Who could make a real difference in keeping the good work going? Advocating for execution means helping your people be the best they can be by coaching, modeling, sharing best practices you have learned, or providing them new tools or professional development opportunities. It may also mean being an advocate for change, continually looking to find a better way to execute.

3. For what can I *lobby*? Champions have to be in it for the long haul. If you see an eventual gain—or an eventual danger, for that matter—you may have to campaign strategically and with determination to make sure progress toward the vision continues on track and on schedule. Championing execution asks you to attend to your persuasive skills, as you work to influence the forward momentum or convince others that the structure you've put in place is the right one.

Doing the Work: Championing Execution

Who or What Can I Defend?	
• What vision-critical person, process, or idea could use a hero right about now? • What kind of defense might the person need in order to complete his or her role successfully?	

For Whom Can I Be a Proponent or Advocate?

- What good work is being done toward making the vision real that is suffering from skepticism or a lack of attention?
- Is there a team, colleague, or concept that could use a cheerleader?
- Who could make a real difference in keeping the good work going?

For What Can I Lobby?

- What potential gain or danger exists that requires me to campaign, persuade, or convince others?

Tips for Momentum

- Lead by example—never ask people for more momentum than you are willing to take on yourself.
- Commit your team to deadlines related to external events.
- Reduce the time between meetings on projects.
- Challenge your priorities to make time for initiating action.
- Focus on choosing the single most important new initiative every day.
- Recognize proactivity and help people see new initiatives as part of their jobs.

Tips for Structure

- Involve the people who will actually be doing the work in the planning process.
- Ensure that plans are robust and sharply focused.
- Expect planning to be an iterative process.
- Create an environment in which there is consistent and timely communication across functions.
- Think critically about what might happen and what has happened.
- Allow time for planning and doing the appropriate analysis.

Tips for Feedback

- Create a culture of candor and trust by acknowledging your own mistakes.
- Have regular, semi-formal dialogues about what isn't working.
- Focus on the problems and not the people.
- Make a conscious effort to prioritize acknowledging people's contributions.
- Make sure your praise is genuine.
- Keep up-to-date on progress and contributions.

Afterword

When the best leader's work is done the people say, "We did it ourselves!"
—Lao-Tsu

In Chapter 1, we told our own company's leadership story of an evolution from chaotic and unproductive to focused and effective. Now it's time to imagine what it might look like to harness the benefits of Vision, Alignment, and Execution in your organization. We want to share some stories of VAE in action, but let's start by giving you a little background.

In 2011, we introduced a leadership development program called Work of Leaders to help leadership training professionals harness the power of the VAE model. Built around a personalized online assessment that in turn generates a personalized *Work of Leaders Profile*, the program helps learners evaluate their current performance in each area identified in the book. Armed with this information, it's easier for learners to apply the simple concepts of Vision, Alignment, and Execution to their work.

During the development of this book, we interviewed current users of the program. We've built three composite vignettes drawn from these interviews to help you imagine what the program looks like in action. As you're reading these vignettes, it's important to understand how the profile helps learners evaluate their current performance in each of the areas discussed in the book. For example, in Chapter 15, we introduced the two drivers of feedback, addressing problems and offering praise. In the profile, the leader sees two continua (as shown in Figure AF.1) that show how inclined she is to address problems and offer praise. In this case, the leader may struggle to speak up about problems in a prompt manner, but may have an easier time remembering to praise people for good work.

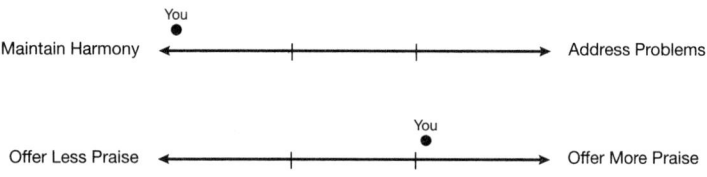

Figure AF.1. Sample Work of Leaders Continua

These vignettes are told from various points of view to give you a broad perspective of approaches and usage. We hope they help you imagine how the VAE model can be useful in your world.

Composite Vignette 1: Individual Coaching

This vignette describes how a coach used Work of Leaders to uncover the source of some of her client's leadership problems. It is told from the perspective of the coach, Barbara, and describes her experience coaching Elaine.

Recently I've been working with Elaine. She works for a multi-national manufacturing company and has moved very quickly from individual contributor to director, but . . . something wasn't working and she couldn't quite put her finger on it. She has a great vision and a really infectious sort of energy, but then nothing happens. And people on her staff are leaving right and left. They hate working for her.

So, after talking things through for a while, I had her take the Work of Leaders assessment online. (This actually took a little prodding.) She scored very high on vision, which wasn't much of a surprise. Remaining open and being bold—those were definite strengths.

We started unearthing the problems when we got to alignment. She was really low on clarity and dialogue. Essentially, when Elaine came up with an idea or concept and gave a project to her team, she didn't even think about dialogue. There was no two-way exchange. She would basically say, "Here's what we're going to do—now let's do it." I pointed out to her that she wasn't creating real alignment with people. She's a global director, so alignment is especially important. She has to deal with people cross-culturally—in China, in Italy, in Brazil, etc. They all need to be on the same page.

> The whole process has been very revealing. It took some time, but slowly the light bulb came on. She started to realize, and own, what the problem was. Her frustration suddenly had some context—the VAE model provided the vocabulary she needed.
>
> And Work of Leaders gave us some really specific areas to focus on during our coaching sessions. We started exploring how Elaine could better explain her rationale, structure her messages, and really slow down to have dialogue with her team. We also plan to extend this experience to her entire staff by having a Work of Leaders session that will include everyone. We hope this will give them a common language to fix some problems.
>
> Really, the whole process was a like a slap upside the head for Elaine, but at just the right stage in her career. This was a constructive approach because we could focus on her strengths, but I could also say, "Now look, if you want to go to the next level, you have to work on building alignment." She knows exactly where to focus her personal development.

Composite Vignette 2: Group Facilitation

This vignette describes part of a Work of Leaders facilitated classroom training session. It is told from the perspective of Sanjeev, who took part in the session. He describes the methods used by the facilitator, Chris, as well as some of the insights gained by participants and their team leader, Anne.

> After we had all looked through our individual Work of Leaders reports, Chris did a really nice job of introducing an

exercise that was pretty eye-opening. He got us up and moving around and placing our dots on those graphs one at a time. We took all the different best practices within Vision, Alignment, and Execution and we charted where everybody was.

As we started to place our dots, we had some informal "aha!" moments where we noticed the whole group was on one side or the other of a particular continuum. But sometimes we were more split—some of us were on one side, and some of us were on the other.

It caused some light-hearted conversation, but then when we stood back and took a couple seconds to just take it all in, we thought, "Wow—as a team, we really have to be careful in a lot of different areas." Some of them were about exploration, where the majority of us were way over to the left, away from the best practice. For example, on remaining open, we didn't really have anyone on the right-hand side.

So Chris went through the same process with our directors, and then with our vice president, Anne. We noticed that a lot of the directors were on one side of the continua and Anne was on the opposite side. And that started a conversation. Because on the one hand you have this VP who is a very energetic people person—you know, all about relationships. And then you have the people on the staff who want closure and try to get stuff done—they don't have those people-focused elements, not naturally anyway. And I know specifically for our group, Anne can see now that our instinct is to jump right to the pros and cons. We want to build the structure and do the analysis right away.

> *I think it really helped Anne understand the work that she has to do as a leader—not only to stretch us, but also to stretch herself. Overall I think it also helped her think, "How can I tap into these groups differently?"*

Composite Vignette 3: Succession Planning

This final vignette describes the thoughts of Maria, a hiring manager who recently participated in a Work of Leaders program. She reflects on the possibilities for using the program to help with succession planning in her organization, as well as some personal insights she gained.

> *I think Work of Leaders is a really interesting tool, and I've had some new thoughts about it in the two weeks since I participated in the seminar. I'm looking at it from the perspective of a hiring organization. We have a mid-level manager training program, and I can easily see this tool as a potential follow-up to that type of program. In that workshop, managers learn about workplace styles and how that impacts their ability to get things done with their teams and across teams within the organization. So it's been very effective and very, very well received.*
>
> *As a follow-up, I see an opportunity to perhaps use VAE in further development and succession planning. If we're putting someone on a succession plan and he or she is going to move into a higher-level leadership position, I think this tool could help us identify development opportunities for this person prior to a move into those roles. Now, one thing our company embodies is continual improvement. If you have*

ideas about bigger and better ways to do things in our organization, then those are valuable leadership abilities around here. So it's important to have vision.

But where it becomes difficult is that you don't really get the alignment or execution because of the ways we do things in our organization. For example, I have to be careful, as someone who's pretty passionate and a big-picture-thinking type, to make sure that I'm not running off into the sunset with these ideas and ignoring all the little steps that I need to take along the way. Am I really having a dialogue and being receptive, to make sure I understand whether people have what they need to get things done? Kind of along the same lines, one of the things I learned is that I have to be careful when I'm communicating my vision—I have a lot of enthusiasm. I'm an optimist and I believe anything can be done, but I work in an industry that's pretty tough. So I have to make sure that I'm not perceived as a Pollyanna because I'm so passionate and enthusiastic about things that I believe in.

Okay, so if we're going to move somebody into a leadership role, especially more strategic and broad-thinking leadership roles, this would be a great tool to (a) find out before we move him or her into that position what his or her development needs are or (b) whether somebody's in a position and is struggling with something, this might shed some light on what we can do to help that individual be more successful.

You know, we put somebody's name in a box on a succession plan. Do we know he is going to be successful in that role?

I think this is a pretty good predictor of the right steps to take to make sure he will be successful.

As these examples show, the VAE model has broad applicability. And when it's applied widely across organizations, it can benefit the whole culture. When the principles of VAE take hold, there's a sense of community and working together toward a common goal. When things go well, there are celebrations. When there are disappointments, people work together to determine what went wrong, without pointing fingers. There's talk about "us," "we," and "together." Everyone realizes he or she is part of something bigger than anyone could have achieved alone.

The Work of Leaders leadership development program is available through our network of professional trainers and consultants. If you're interested in learning more about the program, using the assessment, or tapping into one of our talented consultants to help you bring VAE to life, you'll find information at www.workofleaders.com.

Appendix A: The Development of the Work of Leaders VAE Model

Foundation

Stage 1: Leadership Literature Review

As we explained in Chapter 1, our intent as researchers was not to redefine the concept of leadership, but to make learning about leadership more accessible, particularly in organizational and group settings. We felt confident that not only had the market for pithy aphorisms about leadership been exhausted, but that the heavy lifting of identifying the essence of leadership had been done. However, this meant

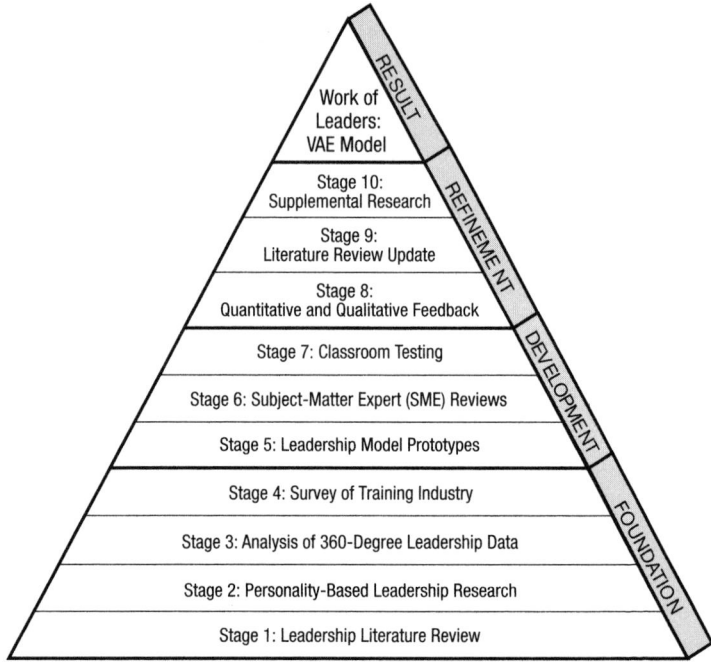

Figure A.1. Work of Leaders Development Pyramid

that we needed to digest and distill the major thinking of the last thirty years of leadership scholarship through review and study of the literature. The books and papers we used as our starting point are listed in the Resources section. We do not claim this to be the definitive collection of authors or books on leadership, but we do believe it represents the majority of the widely recognized and respected thought leaders in the field.

At this point, our primary objective was to identify consistent themes and patterns. We noted points of convergence, and also highlighted exceptions. We also paid special attention to fresh thinking and insights that we felt represented major breakthroughs. Along the way we kept in mind that this information has to be *accessible* if it's going to make a real difference in anyone's work.

Slowly, we were able to see the emergence of patterns. Certain concepts came to the surface again and again. The agreement on the final contents of each bucket of Vision, Alignment, and Execution was an organic process that evolved through the course of the research. But the seeds of our model are readily available in the cumulative body of literature on leadership, accessible to anyone with the time to read and assimilate it all.

Stage 2: Personality-Based Leadership Research

How does personality impact the way we work? We've spent a substantial portion of the last ten years trying to understand this issue. How do forceful managers do their jobs, compared with gentle managers? What traits predict a person's approach to innovation? How long can an extrovert sit alone in his office before he cracks? At Inscape, these are the types of research questions we ask almost constantly. We can quickly show people their strengths, challenges, and blind spots. And it was through this lens that we next studied the topic of leadership.

Take, for example, a study in which we asked leaders which aspect of providing inspiration is most difficult for them. (Recall from Chapter 5 that there are two major aspects of inspiration: being expressive and being encouraging.)

When you first glance at Table A.1, it looks like these two tasks are equally difficult, and you would say there is a 1:1 ratio of leaders who find it difficult to be encouraging or difficult to be expressive. But let's take a look at what happens when we study leaders using a crucial moderating personality

Table A.1. Aspects of Providing Inspiration That Leaders Find Most Difficult

Which behavior is more difficult for you?	
Being expressive	49%
Being encouraging	51%

Table A.2. Aspects of Providing Inspiration That Leaders Find Most Difficult, Based on Personality Factors

Which behavior is more difficult for you?	Leaders with a bold, enterprising personality	Leaders with a cautious, soft-spoken personality
Being expressive	27%	73%
Being encouraging	73%	27%

variable. When we compare leaders who are *enterprising and bold* to leaders who are *cautious and soft-spoken* we get a very different understanding of how leaders behave.

In Table A.2, you can see that there is actually almost a 3:1 preference for being expressive among bold leaders, whereas soft-spoken leaders have a 3:1 preference for being encouraging. Clearly, each of us is going to wrestle with different aspects of leadership.

So how has this approach to leadership research influenced the book you have in your hands? To offer the best possible advice to someone who struggles with "Addressing Problems," we studied people who really *hate* conflict. We worked to understand their need for harmony and their assumptions about being the "bad guy." What do they really fear? As a result of this research, we were able to provide guidance that speaks more directly to leaders who need the most help in this area. We considered what we learned about the people who struggle in a given area and asked, "What does this person really need to hear?"

Because of the work that we do, it's useful to have a blueprint that explains how diverse personalities approach leadership differently. As part of this early research, we constructed twenty-four scales that measure leadership behavior (such as promoting bold action, setting high expectations, facilitating dialogue.) We were then able to look at the relationship among these behaviors. The results of this analysis (called a multidimensional scaling analysis) are shown in Figure A.2. In this figure, behaviors that are closer together have more in common and those farther apart have less in common. Based on this, we can see that people who acknowledge contributions freely are also likely to show enthusiasm and rally people around goals. These people, however, are less likely to speak up about problems or promote disciplined analysis. Armed with this information, we can much more accurately predict the type of feedback that would be helpful to a given individual.

As we progressed through this stage of research, we became more and more interested in understanding the structure of leadership. You can see one such early attempt in Table A.3. Don't worry if this table doesn't make sense to you. The big takeaway is that we found six different themes involved in creating a vision: Boldness, Clarity, Inclusiveness, Risk Management, Consultation, and Realism.

Appendix A

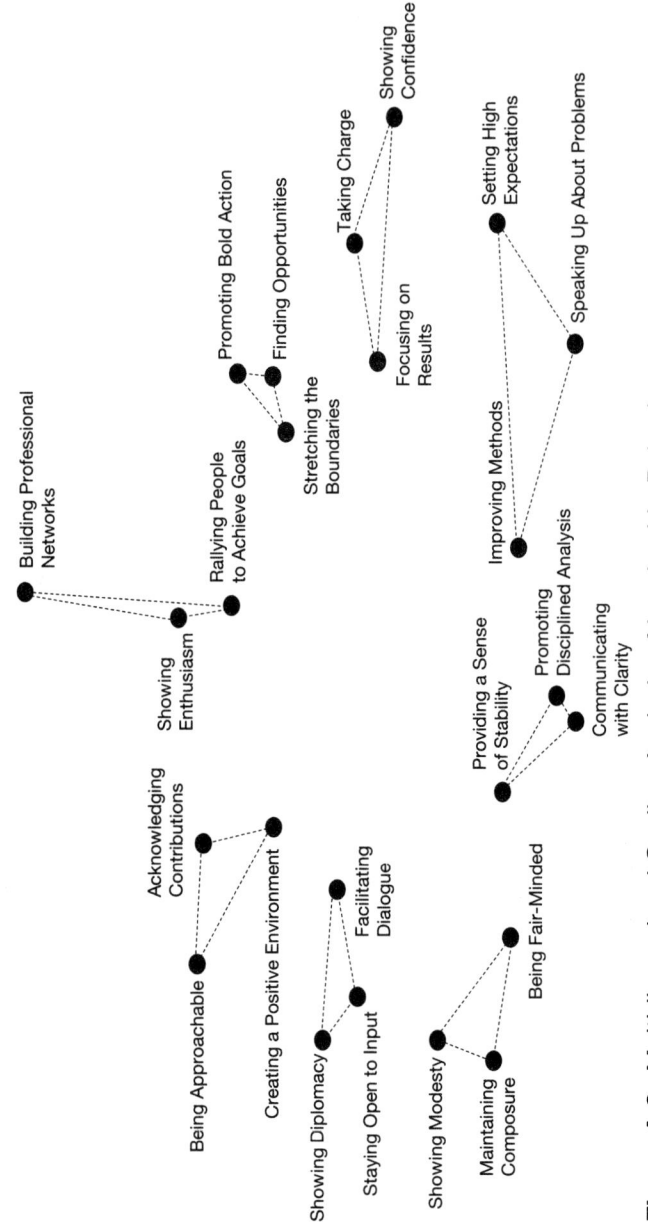

Figure A.2. Multidimensional Scaling Analysis of Leadership Behaviors

Table A.3. Early Factor Analysis of Vision-Related Leadership Behaviors

Item	Factors and Factor Loadings					
	Boldness	Clarity	Inclusiveness	Risk Management	Consultation	Realism
I take chances even if they might seem a little scary to others.	**.82**	.03	.03	.04	−.04	.03
I encourage people to venture into uncharted territory.	**.78**	.06	.10	.03	.04	.02
I pursue adventurous ideas, even if they seem a little risky.	**.77**	−.02	.04	.00	.05	.09
I take on challenges that are bold and daring.	**.76**	.15	.08	.07	−.11	−.02
I encourage people to try things they've never done before.	**.72**	.08	.20	.03	−.02	.01
I tend to challenge the status quo.	**.69**	.10	−.08	.11	.06	.07

Contniued

Table A.3. Continued

Item	Factors and Factor Loadings					
	Boldness	Clarity	Inclusiveness	Risk Management	Consultation	Realism
I encourage others to take risks.	.67	.07	.04	−.09	.26	.05
I tend to take chances with new ideas.	.66	.14	.02	−.06	.16	.00
I defend new ideas, even if they are unpopular.	.49	.14	−.08	.10	.35	.06
I set goals for myself that may seem impossible to others at the time.	.49	.19	.10	.10	−.11	−.06
I make sure that our goals, plans, and direction are not fuzzy.	.03	.69	.09	.26	.20	−.01
I create plans for the group that are focused and crisp.	.14	.66	.20	.24	−.04	.09

Table A.3. Continued

Item	Factors and Factor Loadings					
	Boldness	Clarity	Inclusiveness	Risk Management	Consultation	Realism
I make sure that the group is prioritizing the things that really matter.	.12	**.63**	.17	.24	.05	.11
I encourage the group to make clear, specific choices about where we are headed.	.16	**.63**	.26	.22	−.01	.20
I make sure that we are headed in a direction that is practical and realistic.	.02	**.62**	.17	.13	.10	.11
I push the group to define our goals and plans clearly.	.30	**.61**	−.08	.05	.28	.07
I encourage the group to pinpoint the ideas that are most important.	.16	**.59**	.31	.12	.03	.15

Contniued

Table A.3. Continued

Item	Factors and Factor Loadings					
	Boldness	Clarity	Inclusiveness	Risk Management	Consultation	Realism
I take extra effort to lay out my ideas in a way that it makes sense to people.	.09	**.55**	.27	.19	.08	−.02
I make sure to take everyone's interests into account if I'm developing an idea.	−.02	.11	**.76**	.18	.16	.07
I do my best to generate ideas that everyone can feel good about.	.03	.17	**.72**	.04	.01	.02
I listen for everyone's needs and concerns if I'm developing a plan.	−.02	.15	**.68**	.24	.23	.05
I make sure that the visions I create for the future are appealing to everyone in the group.	.06	.21	**.63**	.02	.05	.15

Table A.3. Continued

Item	Factors and Factor Loadings					
	Boldness	Clarity	Inclusiveness	Risk Management	Consultation	Realism
I make sure that everyone can believe in the direction that the group is headed.	.20	.41	**.57**	.03	.00	.11
I actively work so that other people can picture the ideas and plans as clearly as I do.	.20	.43	**.46**	.17	−.08	.13
I go out of my way to let people know that I am open to feedback on my ideas.	.15	.19	**.45**	.21	.25	−.04
I deliberately look for risks in our plans that we may have overlooked.	.16	.16	.09	**.72**	.03	.15
I take extra time to anticipate potential obstacles.	.08	.29	.24	**.67**	−.06	.06

Contniued

Table A.3. Continued

Item	Factors and Factor Loadings					
	Boldness	Clarity	Inclusiveness	Risk Management	Consultation	Realism
I set aside time to consider the risks involved in new initiatives.	.01	.28	.08	**.65**	.27	.08
I think through all of the consequences of our plans very carefully.	−.06	.36	.08	**.63**	.17	−.04
I actively encourage the group to think through consequences.	.06	.36	.30	**.52**	.02	.23
I make specific efforts to get buy-in from other people if I'm in charge of making plans.	.10	.14	.19	.04	**.70**	.10
I'm deliberately inclusive of everyone's needs if I'm in charge of making plans.	.04	.04	.45	.16	**.52**	.06

Table A.3. Continued

Item	Factors and Factor Loadings					
	Boldness	Clarity	Inclusiveness	Risk Management	Consultation	Realism
I gather input from a wide range of different people when forming my plans.	.07	.17	.27	.36	**.45**	−.10
I urge the group to reconsider whether our plans and goals are really worth doing.	.16	.15	.03	.05	.11	**.79**
I encourage people to reconsider how realistic our vision for the future is.	.10	.27	.25	.15	.00	**.62**
I discourage the group from taking unnecessary risks.	−.26	.10	.15	.32	−.01	**.39**

Results of a principle components factor analysis using a varimax rotation. N = 3,162. Note that factor labels were assigned using the researchers' judgment, attempting to find common themes among the variables loading most highly on a given factor.

The table also shows which behaviors contribute most to each of those themes. As mentioned, this was an early attempt. Eventually, concepts like Clarity and Inclusiveness were shifted into Alignment; Risk Management, Consultation, and Realism were merged into Testing Assumptions; and Boldness was expanded to span both Exploration and Boldness.

We also conducted a series of studies to understand which qualities and behaviors people think are most crucial to successful leadership. In some cases, we explicitly asked them to rate the importance of leadership tasks or to choose from a list the characteristics that are most important for a leader to have. In other cases, we looked at implicit assumptions about leadership. For instance, in one study we had leaders rate another leader in their organization on a number of behaviors (for example, "He/she presents his ideas with passion") as well as on overall effectiveness. From this we were able to see which factors people emphasized most when evaluating the quality of a leader. For instance, we found that experienced leaders (those with twenty or more years of experience) emphasized factors like "setting ambitious goals" and "taking risks" more than inexperienced leaders (those with five or fewer years of experience) did. On the other hand, experienced leaders' ratings were less likely to emphasize behaviors like being structured or highly logical. That is to say, experienced raters were more influenced by the target leader's passion than inexperienced leaders were.

Ultimately, the results of these studies allowed us to create more informed hypotheses about the fundamentals of leadership. It was this background that we would rely on as we began to sketch out the earliest drafts of the VAE model.

Stage 3: Analysis of 360 Leadership Data

Another unique opportunity we have for studying leadership is access to a proprietary database of 360 leadership assessments. The widely used 360-degree feedback tool is particularly valuable for comparing leaders' self-assessments to measurable criteria—ratings from people with different perspectives on the individual leader's effectiveness. Inscape's own 360 assessment, *Everything DiSC 363® for Leaders*, asks people to rate a leader in twenty-four areas. For example, raters are asked to evaluate the leader on statements such as, "She sets high expectations for the group" and "He genuinely listens to other people." Raters also have the chance to ask leaders for specific behavioral changes like: "Acknowledge other people's contributions more." From these responses, we are able to gather a great deal of insight into what direct reports, managers, and peers think about a leader's performance. Consider, for instance, Table A.4, which shows the percentage of raters who asked a leader to perform more of a given behavior.

We can immediately see that certain aspects of vision tend to be requested more often (that is, finding new opportunities, stretching the boundaries). It's also interesting what falls toward the bottom. Relatively few people asked their leaders to show more confidence, which is noteworthy because we often assume that high confidence is a prerequisite to being a leader. Perhaps these people are leaders because they already have high confidence, but our data suggest that there are much more important things for leadership training to focus on. For instance, many more people asked leaders to be more open to input (which may, in fact, be a symptom of over-confidence). It was data like these

Table A.4. Percentage of People Making Requests for Improvement in Their Leaders

Request	Percent of People Making the Request				
	Total	Direct Report	Manager	Peer	Other
Be more active about finding new opportunities	47.2	40.1	63.1	50.3	46.6
Focus more on improving methods	46.1	41.4	58.3	48.4	44.7
Do more to rally people to achieve goals	45.9	40.7	60.3	48.7	43.6
Do more to encourage the group to stretch the boundaries	44.7	34.9	62.8	49.3	44.8
Be more open to input from others	40.9	38.4	47.6	42.8	39.0
Be more active about facilitating dialogue	36.7	31.3	48.0	39.5	35.8
Acknowledge other people's contributions more	36.2	41.6	34.7	33.8	32.6
Create a more positive environment	35.9	35.6	39.9	37.3	33.0
Show more enthusiasm	35.2	29.3	44.9	39.2	34.0
Focus more on setting high expectations	34.1	24.7	50.7	39.2	33.4
Do more to promote bold action in the group	33.5	24.7	48.8	38.2	33.4

Communicate with more clarity	32.0	30.8	41.7	32.5	29.0
Speak up about problems more often	31.6	27.0	39.2	34.2	31.4
Show more diplomacy	31.5	29.3	37.9	33.7	29.1
Work on being more approachable	31.1	31.6	34.2	31.1	29.2
Work more on promoting disciplined analysis	29.5	24.9	42.1	32.2	27.3
Be more active about building personal connections	29.0	22.1	46.3	31.3	28.6
Focus more on results	28.8	20.7	44.6	32.9	28.2
Focus more on taking charge	27.8	19.8	41.1	32.4	27.3
Provide more of a sense of stability	26.9	30.5	26.4	25.9	23.5
Be more fair-minded	24.5	27.6	21.2	24.1	21.9
Maintain his/her composure more effectively	24.0	21.4	31.5	26.3	21.6
Show more confidence	23.2	15.7	37.5	26.6	23.3
Show more modesty	19.3	18.8	18.8	21.3	17.5

N = 81,943. These data were gathered by asking people to give leaders in their organization feedback. The sample contained 27,447 direct reports, 7,904 managers, 19,697 peers, and 26,895 participants classified as others.

that made it clear that one of the nine drivers in the VAE model should be "Dialogue."

As part of our 360 data, we also have access to the comments that people leave for their leaders. In our assessment, participants can choose from almost two hundred developmental comments that they would like to give. In Table A.5, you can see the thirty most commonly used comments. Looking through this list, you find hints about what really matters in leadership and where leaders might want to apply their development efforts. In the right-hand column, you can see which driver in the VAE model addresses a particular comment. For instance, the comment, "He/she could do more to create a motivating environment" is addressed by the Momentum driver. In fact, of the top thirty comments, only one is not directly addressed by the VAE model.

Our 360 assessment also gives raters the opportunity to let us know whether there is something they would like to tell the leader that was not provided in the preselected comments. The information from this "Suggestion Box" helped us to refine our preselected comments, and in the process informed the development of this book. We chose 24,000 unique rater comments from the hundreds of thousands that have been submitted. Reading, analyzing, and categorizing twenty-four buckets of one thousand comments each is obviously a daunting task. However, there is an important upside to this research. First, you're reminded that it's a bit of a wacky world out there. If you're interested in seeing some of the funniest and most creative comments we ran across, take a look at Appendix B. But much more important, by reading through people's frustrations and praises in their own words, you have an extraordinarily rich glimpse of how people really think

Table A.5. Thirty Comments Most Frequently Given to Leaders in Our 360 Survey

Comment	Related Driver
He/she could encourage others to be a bit more creative and adventurous in their thinking.	Exploration Boldness
He/she already works on improving methods, but we would be more effective if he/she did it even more.	Structure
While he/she seems personally driven, he/she doesn't always inspire the same drive in others.	Momentum
He/she could do more to create a motivating environment.	Inspiration Momentum
He/she may not realize that his/her straightforwardness can come across as blunt or aggressive at times.	Dialogue
He/she already acknowledges contributions, but I wish he/she would do it even more often.	Feedback
He/she sometimes seems hesitant to push people beyond their comfort zones.	Momentum
I think he/she could spend more time helping us improve our methods.	Structure
He/she seems to have a decent network but could expand it more.	—
He/she creates a positive environment already, but it would benefit everyone if he/she did it even more often.	Inspiration

Continued

Table A.5. Continued

Comment	Related Driver
He/she sometimes speaks up about problems, but he/she would be even more effective if he/she did it more often.	Feedback
At times, he/she seems to be content with the status quo.	Exploration Momentum
He/she already stretches the boundaries, but he/she would be more effective if he/she did it even more often.	Boldness
He/she could do more to help us see the big picture purpose of what we're doing.	Clarity
He/she already encourages dialogue, but I'd like even more opportunities for us to share our ideas.	Dialogue
He/she sometimes takes charge, but would be even more effective if he/she did it more often.	Momentum
He/she sometimes inspires us, but he/she would be more effective if he/she did it even more often.	Inspiration
He/she's very efficient, and I wish he/she would use that talent to help others improve their methods.	Structure
He/she is in a unique position to inspire people.	Inspiration
He/she doesn't always seem to recognize our frustration with inefficiencies.	Structure

Table A.5. Continued

Comment	Related Driver
He/she already focuses on results, but he/she would be more effective if he/she did it even more often.	Momentum
At times, he/she seems a little uncomfortable about speaking up when there's a problem.	Feedback
He/she's not necessarily the cause of the instability in our organization, but he/she could do more to fix it.	Structure Clarity
He/she sometimes prefers to just keep doing things the way we always have.	Exploration Boldness
He/she sometimes doesn't give consideration to all sides of an issue.	Testing Assumptions Dialogue
He/she already promotes bold action, but it would be great if he/she did it even more often.	Boldness
His/her diplomacy sometimes suffers when he/she is under stress.	Dialogue
It would be helpful if he/she would address issues more directly and candidly.	Feedback
During disagreements, he/she sometimes spends more time making his/her points than listening to others.	Dialogue
He/she doesn't always seem aware of the contributions we make.	Feedback

This list reflects the comments most frequently given to leaders. In total, 185 different comments were used, and comments were given 113,421 times. This list only includes comments that reflect a need for improvement, as opposed to comments that reflect praise.

about their leaders. Again, our goal was to use these insights to connect with our readers.

Stage 4: Survey of Training Industry

Over a period of three years, from 2009 to 2011, we conducted nineteen separate studies on training in organizations, the results of which were published in regular columns in *Training* magazine. From these studies we came to understand a great deal about how learners think about leadership. For instance, we learned that leadership is by far the most desired topic in corporate training. We were able to find out what percentage of workers think of themselves as leaders in their organizations. We also found that the vast majority of workers consider themselves to have at least decent leadership skills, regardless of their formal titles. As shown in Table A.6, we clarified what experiences have most shaped the development of our leaders.

The results of inquiries like these helped us better understand our audience and how these learners think about their development as leaders. This information, in turn, was crucial as we began to think about what type of learning model would be most helpful for both new and seasoned leaders.

Development

Stage 5: Leadership Model Prototypes

Armed with these four major inputs, our design team set out to capture the essential responsibilities of leaders in the simplest framework possible. We went through numerous iterations, working to make the model straightforward and accessible to everyone in the organization.

Table A.6. Experiences and Sources That Have Most Shaped Leaders' Development

Experience/Source	Percent of Respondents Who Selected This Item
Work experience (non-management)	74
Management experience	59
Being a parent/guardian	45
A mentor	42
Leadership training	41
A family role model	40
A manager	39
Academic work	29
Experience in athletics	28
Reading about leadership	26
A role model (non-family)	26
Community work	25
A specific life experience (non-work)	22
Training (non-leadership)	22
Teaching	22
School activities (non-athletic)	22
Work within a religious institution	17
An athletic coach	14
I don't really have leadership skills	2
None of the above	1

Our emphasis at this stage was connecting the theories with the learners, helping people see themselves in the model and the narrative. To that end, we used M. David Merrill's *First Principles of Instruction* as a lens for developing our learning design. Merrill offers a conceptual framework focused around problem-centered instruction that includes four phases—activation, demonstration, application, and integration. Most specifically, we began with Merrill's "Activation Principle" as a starting point, and we looked for ways to tie to people's prior experience by finding words in the model that people could really relate to. This started with the highest level concepts of Vision, Alignment, and Execution, but it also applied all the way through the model to the words we used for drivers and best practices.

Stage 6: Subject-Matter Expert (SME) Reviews

With our initial leadership models in hand, we approached a few hundred of the 1,800 independent trainers, business coaches, and consultants in Inscape's Network. We're extremely fortunate that these professionals are always willing to share their expertise with us. They have also been generous in giving us access to many of their biggest clients, which include almost half of the Fortune 500 companies, thousands of mid-sized and small businesses, as well as many of the largest governmental agencies, educational institutions, and non-profit organizations. As a result, we were able to interview hundreds of highly experienced HR professionals who reviewed and critiqued our leadership model prototypes, which gradually evolved into the final VAE model.

Stage 7: Classroom Testing

The Work of Leaders VAE model has been heavily influenced by our experience with classroom learners. Our position as one of the world's largest suppliers of assessment-based classroom learning solutions provided us another exceptional opportunity to refine and evaluate leadership models and optimize the learning experience. When we develop a new classroom learning program, we conduct, on average, four or five rounds of field testing with dozens of organizations and hundreds of participants, allowing about two months for each round to be completed.

Refinement

Stage 8: Quantitative and Qualitative Feedback

After the training sessions, we ask the classroom facilitators and the learners to complete an online survey to give us feedback on their experience. What was insightful for them? What was confusing? We also conduct one-hour, in-depth phone interviews with the consultants and trainers about what worked in their sessions and what did not.

We then spend weeks making revisions based on the feedback—then we test again. We mention this process here because it was crucial in shaping the development of the VAE model. The "eureka moment" in this lengthy process was when we recognized how quickly learners grasped onto the idea of *Vision, Alignment,* and *Execution*. People called them "magic words." Although none of the words was new to them, organizing leadership in this way was at once simple and compelling. It consistently spurred meaningful conversations about both individual and group leadership strengths and challenges. We also learned that some of our original drivers—one level down in the model—were not as meaningful or clear as others. In some cases, the feedback pointed to a simple need to wordsmith (for example, "momentum" applies more broadly than "urgency"). In other cases, however, it became evident that we needed to revisit a basic concept that we were measuring and teaching (for example, "structuring messages" is more critical to clarity than "being succinct").

Stage 9: Literature Review Update

Over the course of our five years developing the VAE model, we were introduced to a wealth of additional leadership material. Perhaps just as important, however, we encountered thought leaders who were not speaking directly about leadership, but still had a great deal to contribute to the leadership conversation. Researchers like Daniel Kahneman and Robert Zajonc most prominently address topics in economics and psychology, but ultimately they are describing patterns that govern how we think, feel, and act in a variety of different arenas, including leadership.

At this stage, then, our goal was to pull together all of these disparate sources and understand how they relate to each other and to the VAE framework. Similarly, we recognized the need to look at outside models of individual and group behavior (for example, Patrick Lencioni's pyramid from *The Five Dysfunctions of a Team*) and investigate how they align with the VAE model. Ultimately, we worked to synthesize knowledge from a variety of different disciplines that could inform the art and practice of crafting a vision, building alignment, and championing execution.

Stage 10: Supplemental Research

Once the VAE model had crystallized, we spent time exploring various aspects of vision, alignment, and execution more deeply. For instance, while researching alignment, we found that both experienced and inexperienced leaders indicated that, within the VAE model, the area they struggled with most was alignment. We wondered just what this concept ("getting alignment") means to the average leader. Tables A.7 and A.8 show two of the questions we were able to quickly ask.

We were surprised. It became evident that there really is not much formal discussion of alignment in organizations. Leaders are receiving very little guidance. This knowledge helped us understand that we had to spend more time explaining the fundamentals of alignment to leaders.

Table A.7. Alignment Follow-Up Question 1

In your leadership development, how much training or guidance have you had in the practice of getting alignment?	
	Percent
None or almost none	26
A little bit	39
A fair amount	26
A lot	4
A great deal	5

Table A.8. Alignment Follow-Up Question 2

How clear an understanding do you feel you have of what "getting alignment" means in the context of leadership?	
	Percent
Very unclear	4
Vague idea	23
Decent understanding	25
Pretty clear understanding	39
Extremely clear understanding	8

The Result: Vae Model

Ultimately, all of the methods and resources described here were used to build the VAE model seen in Figure 1.1 (in Chapter 1) and explained throughout this book. Obviously, one of our top priorities was accuracy. We wanted to make sure that our model reflected what really matters in leadership. But equally important was the priority we discussed in Chapter 1—accessibility. The biggest contribution we felt we could make to the field of leadership development was making what is known about the work of leaders accessible as a common language to develop more effective leadership—both for the individual and for the organization. Fortunately, the reactions we have received to VAE since the release of the Work of Leaders program suggest that we have achieved our objective. It's our sincere hope that this model will resonate with you and others in your organization as well.

Appendix B: Feedback Outtakes

As noted in the first chapter of this book, we conducted dozens of studies over the past five years with hundreds of thousands of participants. With that number of respondents, you can imagine the broad array of feedback we received, especially when the participants had a chance to use their own words to voice their opinions about their leaders. On the whole, the responses were honest, insightful, and telling. They were also often funny.

We've collected some of our favorite gems, and it seemed a pity not to share them—not only because the responses may make you laugh, but also because they can offer real insight into the types of concerns people have regarding their leaders. The following are just a few of the responses people submitted. All names and personally identifiable information have been changed.

- Don exhibits qualities that are similar to those of Indiana Jones.
- She is very selfish and really does not like to give credit to people she does not like, which is virtually everyone.
- He should be here more often instead of constantly being off riding his motorcycle.
- Molly is like a scale of justice.
- Could at least learn names and job descriptions of folks who call him "boss."
- She needs to learn to eat shrimp products without overreacting.
- He never tells me how awesome I am.
- People seek her out for advice. Maybe sometimes she is too approachable and people dump on her.
- Only problem with Matt is he only works eleven hours a day.
- Dan is an in-your-face kind of guy who does not understand the meaning of personal space.
- The cheerleader outfit was a bit too much.
- If Clint were any more approachable, he may literally have to be a teddy bear.
- It's more of a Jekyll and Hyde sort of thing. Which Audrey will be at work today? The fairly easygoing Audrey who can be very enjoyable company and open to suggestions or thoughts? Or will it be the don't talk to me, look at me, or especially not talk to me Audrey who is off on some dark planet of her own?

- Whenever on the phone with him regarding a work issue he has had to put me on hold to either discipline his children or his dog.
- She has mastered the art of being a bully. She is the consummate Machiavellian and engages in the art of the personal destruction of others.
- The only thing that I have learned from him is how to avoid him.
- Fair-minded is Lydia's middle name.
- Can't get a logical answer out of him most of the time. Ask a simple question and you end up walking away baffled and with a migraine.
- She calls herself a Type A personality. I think that's a euphemism for "I don't know how to build relationships."
- He'll reply with "yes" after you've asked him six questions.
- Claudia is a great communicator. Her nonverbals also speak volumes.
- Stop throwing my shoes into the woods.
- If Suzy were any more positive and supportive, she'd be a plus sign.
- Once we were told as a group in an email that we "suck."
- You just cringe when you get called to her office.
- If there was a big chalkboard with "YOU'RE LATE" "HURRY UP" "WHY ISN'T IT DONE?" written on it, it would save them time in repetition. We could just refer to the board.
- She is bossy in an email, but then jokes about her cat the next minute.
- If Google says to do it, she will.
- HE GETS HIMSELF AND THE COMPANY BOGGED DOWN BY OVERANALYZING!!!!!! Capital letters and

exclamation points were intentionally added to underscore the point.
- Nothing against Stephanie personally, I just don't think she has the knowledge, skills, abilities, or experience.
- If there is an earthquake, I wanna be near Mr. Stable.
- If the chaotic universe represented our workplace, then Karen would be the sun in our solar system that held the planets in gravitational orbit. I honestly believe that most people would buckle under the amount of pressure and stress that Karen has to deal with every day. Either that, or scream in the car on the way back home every day after work. The very fact that our department can function day to day is a tribute to her skill in maintaining order and stability. I'd give her the Nobel Peace Prize if I had one. I simply don't know how she does it.
- How about: He encourages the highest level of achievement by actively encouraging his employees to reach their goals. Then I could check no.
- She literally makes people cry.
- WE ARE ADULTS AND THE WOOP-WOOP DOES NOT MAKE US PERFORM BETTER.
- When Jeffrey is passionate about a project, his sense of enthusiasm is indeed contagious; sometimes I get a rash.
- She is like poison in this office.
- I do not need anyone ringing cow bells, wearing silly hats, or throwing me candy.
- Shanda is like the rock of Gibraltar.

References

Amabile, T. (2012). Componential theory of creativity [Abstract]. Harvard Business School. Retrieved from http://hbswk.hbs.edu/item/7011.html.

Blanchard, K. (n.d.). Critical leadership skills: Key traits that can make or break today's leaders. Retrieved from www.kenblanchard.com/img/pub/pdf_critical_ leadership_skills.pdf.

Bossidy, L., & Charan, R. (2002). *Execution: The discipline of getting things done*. New York: Crown Business.

Buckingham, M. (2005). *The one thing you need to know*. New York: The Free Press.

Carrere, S., & Gottman, J. (1999). Predicting divorce among newlyweds from the first three minutes of a marital conflict discussion. *Family Process 38*(3), 293–301.

Christensen, C. (1997). *The innovator's dilemma: The revolutionary book that will change the way you do business*. New York: HarperBusiness.

Collins, J. (2001). *Good to great: Why some companies make the leap . . . and others don't*. New York: HarperCollins.

Galton, F. (1907). Vox Populi. *Nature, 1949*(75), 450–451.

Gilbert, D. (2006). *Stumbling on happiness*. New York: Knopf.

Godin, S. (2008). *Tribes: We need you to lead us*. New York: Portfolio Hardcover.

Goleman, D., Boyatzis, R., & McKee, A. (2001, December). Primal leadership: The hidden driver of great performance. *Harvard Business Review, 79*(11), 42–51.

Goleman, D., Boyatzis, R., & McKee, A. (2004). *Primal leadership: Learning to lead with emotional intelligence*. Boston: Harvard Business Press.

Gottman, J. (1994). *Why marriages succeed or fail: . . . and how you can make yours last*. New York: Simon & Schuster.

Hsieh, T. (2010). *Delivering happiness: A path to profits, passion, and purpose*. New York: Business Plus.

Kahneman, D. (2011). *Thinking, fast and slow*. New York: Farrar, Straus and Giroux.

Kelley, T. (2005). *The ten faces of innovation: IDEO's strategies for beating the devil's advocate and driving creativity throughout your organization*. New York: Doubleday.

Kotter, J. (1996). *Leading change*. Boston: Harvard Business Review Press.

Klein, G. (2004). *The power of intuition: How to use your gut feelings to make better decisions at work*. New York: Crown Business.

Kouzes, J.M., & Posner, B.Z. (2002). *The leadership challenge*. San Francisco: Jossey-Bass.

Kraemer, H. (2011). *From values to action*. San Francisco: Jossey-Bass.

Langer, E., Blank, A., & Chanowitz, B. (1978). The mindlessness of ostensibly thoughtful action: The role of "placebic" information in interpersonal interaction. *Journal of Personality and Social Psychology*, 36(6), 635–542.

Lencioni, P. (2012). *The advantage: Why organizational health trumps everything else in business*. San Francisco: Jossey-Bass.

Lencioni, P. (2002). *The five dysfunctions of a team*. San Francisco: Jossey-Bass.

Levitt, T. (1960). Marketing myopia. *Harvard Business Review*, 38(4), 45–56.

Logan, D., King, J., & Fischer-Wright, H. (2008). *Tribal leadership: Leveraging natural groups to build a thriving organization*. New York: HarperBusiness.

Maxwell, J. (1998). *The 21 irrefutable laws of leadership: Follow them and people will follow you*. Nashville, TN: Thomas Nelson.

McGregor, D. (1960). *The human side of enterprise*. New York: McGraw-Hill.

Merrill, D. (2013). *First principles of instruction*. San Francisco: Pfeiffer.

Norman, S., Avolio, B., & Luthans, F. (2010). The impact of positivity and transparency on trust in leaders and their perceived effectiveness. *The Leadership Quarterly*, 21(3), 350–364.

Patterson, K., Grenny, J., Maxfield, D., McMillan, R., & Switzler, A. (2012). *Change anything: The new science of personal success*. New York: Business Plus.

Peters, T., & Waterman, R. (2004). *In search of excellence: Lessons from America's best-run companies*. New York: HarperBusiness.

Roets, A., & van Hiel, A. (2008). Why some hate to dilly-dally and others do not: The arousal-invoking capacity of decision-making for low- and high-scoring need for closure individuals. *Social Cognition*, 26(3), 333–346.

Senge, P. (1990). *The fifth discipline: The art and practice of the learning organization*. New York: Doubleday.

Wooden, J., & Jamison, S. (2005). *Wooden on leadership: How to create a winning organization*. New York: McGraw-Hill.

Wren, D., Bedeian, A., & Breeze, J. (2002). The foundations of Henri Fayol's administrative theory. *Management Decision*, *40*(9), 906–918.

Zajonc, R. B. (2003). *The selected works of R.B. Zajonc*. Hoboken, NJ: John Wiley & Sons.

Zizek, S. (1992). *Looking awry: An introduction to Jacques Lacan through popular culture*. Cambridge, MA; MIT Press.

Resources

Bardwick, J. (1996). Peacetime management and wartime leadership. In F. Hesselbein, M. Goldsmith, & R. Beckhard (Eds.), *The leader of the future: New visions, strategies, and practices for the next era* (pp. 131–139). San Francisco: Jossey-Bass.

Bennis, W. (2003). *On becoming a leader.* New York: Basic Books.

Bossidy, L., & Charan, R. (2002). *Execution: The discipline of getting things done.* New York: Crown Business.

Carlson Nelson, M., & Cundy, D. (2008). *How we lead matters: Reflections on a life in leadership.* New York: McGraw-Hill.

Center for Creative Leadership. (2003). Leadership skills and emotional intelligence. Retrieved September 3, 2009, from www.ccl.org/leadership/pdf/assessments/skills_intelligence.pdf.

Cohn, J., & Moran, J. (2011). *Why are we bad at picking good leaders?* San Francisco: Jossey-Bass.

Coutu, D. (2009). Leadership lessons from Abraham Lincoln: A conversation with historian Doris Kearns Goodwin. *Harvard Business Review, 87*(4), 43–47.

Covey, S. (1996). Three roles of the leader in the new paradigm. In F. Hesselbein, M. Goldsmith, & R. Beckhard (Eds.), *The leader of the future: New visions, strategies, and practices for the next era* (pp. 149–159). San Francisco: Jossey-Bass.

De Pree, Max. (2004). *Leadership is an art.* New York: Crown Business.

Drucker, P. (1985). *Innovation and entrepreneurship.* New York: HarperBusiness.

Drucker, P. (1999). *Management challenges for the 21st century.* New York: HarperBusiness.

Drucker, P. (2008). *The essential Drucker: The best of sixty years of Peter Drucker's essential writings on management.* New York: Harper Paperbacks.

Duffy, G. (2006). Being a visionary leader. [Commencement address]. Retrieved from www.commonwealthclub.org/gloriaduffy/column-archive/USF CommencementSpeech.pdf.

Gebelein, S., Lee, D., Nelson-Neuhaus, K., & Sloan, E. (2000). *Successful executive's handbook: Development suggestions for today's executives.* Minneapolis: Personnel Decisions International.

Godin, S. (2008). *Tribes: We need you to lead us.* New York: Portfolio Hardcover.

Goleman, D., Boyatzis, R., & McKee, A. (2001, December). Primal leadership: The hidden driver of great performance. *Harvard Business Review, 79*(11), 42–51.

Goleman, D., Boyatzis, R., & McKee, A. (2004). *Primal leadership: Learning to lead with emotional intelligence.* Boston: Harvard Business Press.

Goodwin, D.K. (2005). *Team of rivals: The political genius of Abraham Lincoln.* New York: Simon & Schuster.

Greenleaf, R. (2002). *Servant leadership: A journey into the nature of legitimate power and greatness.* New York: Paulist Press.

Hackman, J. (2005). Rethinking team leadership *or* team leaders are not music directors. In D. Messick & R. Kramer (Eds.), *The psychology of leadership: New perspectives and research*. Mahwah, NJ: Lawrence Erlbaum Associates.

Hesselbein, F. (2002). *Hesselbein on leadership*. San Francisco: Jossey-Bass.

Hesselbein, F., Goldsmith, M., & Beckhard, R. (Eds.). (1996). *The leader of the future: New visions, strategies, and practices for the next era*. San Francisco: Jossey-Bass.

Hsieh, T. (2010). *Delivering happiness: A path to profits, passion, and purpose*. New York: Business Plus.

Irwin, T. (2009). *De-railed: Five lessons learned from catastrophic failures of leadership*. Nashville, TN: Thomas Nelson.

Kahnweiler, J. (2009). *The introverted leader*. San Francisco: Berrett-Koehler.

Kotter, J. (1998). What leaders really do. In *Harvard Business Review on leadership*. Boston: Harvard Business School Publishing.

Kotter, J. (2007). Leading change: Why transformation efforts fail. *Harvard Business Review, 85*(1), 96–103.

Kouzes, J.M., & Posner, B.Z. (2002). *The leadership challenge*. San Francisco: Jossey-Bass.

Logan, D., King, J., & Fischer-Wright, H. (2008). *Tribal leadership: Leveraging natural groups to build a thriving organization*. New York: HarperBusiness.

Maxwell, J. (2007). *The 21 irrefutable laws of leadership: Follow them and people will follow you*. Nashville, TN: Thomas Nelson.

Messick, D. (2005). On the psychological exchange between leaders and followers. In D. Messick & R. Kramer (Eds.), *The psychology of leadership: New perspectives and research*. Mahwah, NJ: Lawrence Erlbaum Associates.

Patterson, K., Grenny, J., McMillian, R., & Switzler, A. (2002). *Crucial conversations: Tools for talking when the stakes are high*. New York: McGraw-Hill.

Pinchot, G. (1996). Creating organizations with many leaders. In F. Hesselbein, M. Goldsmith, & R. Beckhard (Eds.), *The leader of the future: New visions, strategies, and practices for the next era* (pp. 25–39). San Francisco: Jossey-Bass.

Pink, D. (2011). *Drive: The surprising truth about what motivates us.* New York: Riverhead Trade.

Rath, T., & Conchie, B. (2008). *Strengths based leadership.* New York: Gallup Press.

Schein, E. (1992). Leadership and organizational culture. In F. Hesselbein, M. Goldsmith, & R. Beckhard (Eds.), *The leader of the future: New visions, strategies, and practices for the next era* (pp. 59–69). San Francisco: Jossey-Bass.

Senge, P. (1990). *The fifth discipline: The art and practice of the learning organization.* New York: Doubleday.

Tzu, S. (L. Giles, Ed. & Trans.). (2007). *The art of war.* Ann Arbor, MI: Borders Classics.

Welch, J. (2005). *Winning.* New York: HarperCollins.

Wiseman, L., & McKeown, G. (2010). *Multipliers: How the best leaders make everyone smarter.* New York: HarperBusiness.

Wooden, J., & Jamison, S. (2005). *Wooden on leadership: How to create a winning organization.* New York: McGraw-Hill.

Zenger, J., & Folkman, J. (2007). *The handbook for leaders: 24 lessons for extraordinary leadership.* New York: McGraw-Hill.

About Inscape Publishing

Acquired by John Wiley & Sons, Inc., in February 2012, Inscape Publishing, Inc., is a leading developer of DiSC®-based corporate training and assessment solutions. Inscape recently launched Everything DiSC®, its third-generation applications that combine online assessment, classroom facilitation, and post-training follow-up reports to create powerful, personalized workplace development experiences.

With a global network of nearly 1,800 independent trainers, coaches, and consultants, Inscape's solution-focused products are used in thousands of organizations, including major government agencies and Fortune 500 companies. Every year, more than one million people worldwide participate in programs that use an Inscape assessment. Inscape products have been translated into thirty different languages and are used in seventy countries.

About the Authors

For more than ten years, the authors have worked together at Inscape Publishing to create training products that help organizations, facilitators, and learners get the most out of the time they invest in workplace development. Our team is committed to the belief that leadership and learning can transform the way organizations work.

We each come at our jobs differently, but one thing we share is that we get to come to the office every day, work with people we respect and admire, and do what we love. As authors, we are privileged to represent the work that has been accomplished by everyone at Inscape.

About the Authors

Julie Straw oversees Inscape's network of more than 1,800 trainers, coaches, and consultants. When writing our chapter on inspiration, we had no better role model than Julie. Her ability to connect and engage people is one reason why so many leaders have been able to profit from the research in this book. She has a genuine talent for taking a new idea and helping people see how it can make a difference in their lives. Julie is a frequent speaker at national conferences and seminars, and is author of *The 4-Dimensional Manager*.

Mark Scullard, Ph.D., leads all aspects of research for Inscape, including research strategies, data analysis, and the development of psychological assessments. His creativity and passion for making learning stick have compelled him to expand his contributions far beyond psychometrics, and you can find Mark's trademark humor and gift for creating simple, memorable models throughout Inscape's products. Mark's research has been published in both academic and trade journals, and he is co-author of *The 8 Dimensions of Leadership*.

Susie Kukkonen leads all product development efforts at Inscape. Susie has the monumental distinction of bringing closure to an R&D team that thrives on last-minute changes. There are few people who can stay completely open to new innovations and simultaneously keep a detailed eye on a quality and deadlines. Susie is one of them. With a focus on constant improvement, she ensures that every program we make is better than the last.

About the Authors

Barry Davis oversees both marketing and product development for Inscape. As much as we've spent the whole book disclaiming visionary leadership, Barry is our visionary. He enjoys the role of questioning assumptions and driving innovation, and when we wrote the chapter on momentum, we had Barry in mind. His passion for delivering results by gaining a deep understanding of customer needs has led to a new generation of highly valued products.

Index

Page references followed by *fig* indicate an illustrated figure; followed by *t* indicate a table.

A

Accessibility: need for information, 2–3; as VAE model priority, 188; as vision for leadership, 8–9

"Activation Principle" concept, 184

Addressing problems: leaders' self-ratings on, 137*t*; Pixar "crit" sessions, 138; "political factors" barrier to, 139*t*; providing feedback by, 138–140; strategies for, 140–142; studying people who hate conflict to examine, 164–165; survey on what keeps you from speaking up about, 139*t*

Alignment: all levels of, 66–67; conserves time and energy, 65; as dynamic and ongoing process, 63–64; lesson on the importance of, 61–62; provides a forum for questions and concerns, 65–66; Supplemental Research follow-up question 1 on, 187*t*; Supplemental Research follow-up question 2 on, 188*t*; unites and excites people around a vision, 66; what we mean by, 62–65. *See also* Building Alignment

Amabile, T., 111

Ambition, 117

American Society for Training and Development (ASTD), 116

Analysis of 360-Degree Leadership Data: description of, 6*t*; percentage of people making requests for improvement in their leaders, 176*t*–177*t*; VAE model development based on the, 175–182; Work of Leaders

207

Index

Development Pyramid position of, 162*fig*. *See also* Leader surveys
Analyzing in-depth: benefit of taking the time for, 131–132; building structure through, 131–132; strategies for, 132–133
Audience: "audience effect" of exchanging perspectives in front of, 83; Building Alignment by knowing your, 100–101, 102–103; how the "gaze of the audience" beliefs impact behavior, 84. *See also* Team members
"Audience effect," 83
Avolio, B., 74

B

Beckett, Jack, 53–54, 54
Behaviors. *See* Leadership behaviors
Being adventurous: boldness component of, 36–37; strategies for, 37–38
Being driven: gaining momentum by, 116–118; inexperienced leaders' insecurity as barrier to, 117–118; leaders who set high or low expectations, 117–118*t*; "Model the Way" for, 119; strategies for, 118–120
Being encouraging: comparing positive feedback to, 94; creating inspiration by, 94–95; as difficult aspect of providing inspiration, 164*t*; as difficult aspect of providing inspiration based on personality factors, 164*t*; strategies for, 95–96; tapping into their motivation for, 96
Being expressive: characteristics of, 92; as difficult aspect of providing inspiration, 164*t*; as difficult aspect of providing inspiration based on personality factors, 164*t*; providing inspiration by, 91–92; strategies for, 92–93; "talking points" for, 93
Being receptive: engaging in dialogue by, 80, 84–87; feedback from real people on, 85–86; strategies for, 87–88; vulnerability exercise to build trust for, 86–87
Bennis, Warren: on distinctions between management and leadership, 126; on guiding vision of leadership, 53; on leadership as capacity to realize a vision, 1; perspective on leadership by, 4
Berra, Yogi, 20
BHAG ("Big Hairy Audacious Goal"), 20
"Bias for action" concept, 114
Body language: being expressive through your, 93; verifying your receptiveness through your, 87, 88
Boldness: being adventurous component of, 36–38; comments from 360 survey on, 179*t*, 180*t*, 181*t*; as driving Crafting a Vision, 9*fig*; expanded to include Exploration, 174; innovation as crucial element of, 33–34; leaders' reasons given for lack of, 34–35*fig*; resistance to, 34; speaking out component of, 35, 38–41; stretching the boundaries to exercise, 34–36; tips for, 41, 57; as vision-related leadership behavior, 165, 167*t*–173*t*
Bossidy, Larry: *Execution: The Discipline of Getting Things Done* co-authored by, 126–127; leadership perspective of, 4
Buckingham, Marcus: leadership perspective of, 4; *The One Thing You Need to Know* by, 95
Building Alignment: as act of gaining buy-in for your vision, 62; additional guidelines for, 100–102; Clarity driver of, 9*fig*, 69–77, 80; Dialogue driver of, 9*fig*, 79–88; Doing the Work for, 102–104; as essential to project success, 67; importance and benefits of, 65–66; Inspiration

driver of, 9*fig*, 89–97; as people-centered part of the VAE model, 99–100; VAE model on leader responsibility for, 5, 8. *See also* Alignment
Building Alignment benefits: alignment conserves time and energy, 65; provides a forum for questions and concerns, 65–66; unites and excites people around a vision, 66
Building Alignment guidelines: continuously build alignment, 101–102; know your audience, 100–101, 102–103; practice the skills, 101
Buy-in: Building Alignment in order to gain, 62; exchanging perspectives in order to gain, 83; inspiration use gaining, 90. *See also* Credibility

C
Card game feedback, 135–136
Championing Execution: at all levels, 111–112; Doing the Work of, 149–151; Feedback driver of, 9*fig*, 135–146, 151; importance of, 109–111; Momentum driver of, 9*fig*, 113–123, 150; questions to ask about, 148–159; Structure driver of, 9*fig*, 125–134, 150–151; VAE model on leader responsibility for, 5, 8, 107–108, 109. *See also* Execution
Championing Execution benefits: assuring development of concrete strategies, 110–111; gives people a sense of achievement, 111; tangible sign of leader commitment, 110
Championing Execution questions: for what can I lobby?, 149; for whom can I be a proponent or advocate?, 148–149; who or what can I defend?, 148
Champions: characteristics of, 109; Doing the Work of Championing Execution, 149–151; establishing and defining credibility as, 110; questions to ask about being a, 148–149
Change: Change + Uncertainty = Chaos formula for, 147; creating a sense of urgency for, 115; momentum during times of, 115; New opportunities for, 24–29, 120–123
Change + Uncertainty = Chaos formula, 73
Change Anything (Patterson and others), 147
Charan, Ram, 127
Christensen, Clayton, 33
Clarity: comments from 360 survey on, 180*t*, 181*t*; comments given to leaders about need for more, 70–71*t*; crisp communication used for, 69–70; as driving Building Alignment, 9*fig*; explaining rationale component of, 72–75; know your audience questions to ask about, 101, 102; monitoring for comprehension for, 74–75; one-way communication required for, 80; as requiring context, 70; shifted into Alignment with Inclusiveness, 174; structuring messages for, 75–76; tips for, 77, 103; as vision-related leadership behavior, 165, 167*t*–173*t*
Classroom Testing, 6*t*
Collaborative Work of Leaders, 10
Collins, Jim, 4, 20
"Common enemy" strategies, 95–96
Communication: Building Alignment through clarity of, 9*fig*, 69–77, 80; creating an environment with consistent and timely, 133; different styles of leadership, 71–72; importance of emotional and rational alignment, 64; nonverbal body language, 87, 88, 93; power of crisp, 69–70; providing context for, 70;

transparent, 74, 135–136; Xerox line experiment on explaining rationale, 72. *See also* Dialogue; Information; Messages

Comprehension, 74–75

Conflict: study of people who hate, 164–165; training people to resolve, 3*t*

Conflict resolution: interest in training to improve skills for, 3*t*; understanding the need for harmony and, 164–165

Consultation: merged into Testing Assumptions, 174; as vision-related leadership behavior, 165, 167*t*–173*t*

Cornerstone Principles of Work of Leaders, 10

Corning's Gorilla Glass, 108

Crafting a Vision: at all levels, 21–22; Boldness driver of, 9*fig*, 33–41; Doing the Work for, 56–57; doing the work steps for, 56–57; Exploration driver of, 9*fig*, 23–32; as a human skill, 13–14; importance of, 17–21; learning the skills of, 54–56; as the most conceptual part of VA model, 62; Testing Assumptions driver of, 9*fig*, 43–51; the Transamerica Pyramid example of, 53–54; VAE model on leader responsibility for, 5, 8. *See also* Vision

Crafting a Vision benefits: drives the creation of goals, 20; helps us stand out from our competitors, 20; provides purpose, 20

Crafting a Vision reminders: choose the scope, 55; find the right balance, 55; trust the process, 55–56

Crafting a Vision Work: find the right balance, 56; know the scope of the vision you're crafting, 56; tips for boldness, 41, 57; tips for exploration, 31–32, 56; tips for testing assumptions, 50–51, 57

Credibility: establishing and defining champion's, 110; when being too optimistic threatens our, 95. *See also* Buy-in

Crisp communication, 69–70

"Criti" sessions, 138

"Cross-docking" practice (Wal-Mart), 108

Curie, Marie, 15

D

Darwin, Charles, 50

De Press, Max, 4

Dialogue: being receptive component of, 80, 84–88; comments from 360 survey on, 179*t*, 180*t*, 181*t*; *dia-logos* (through and word or meaning) origins of, 79–80; differentiating between discussion and, 79; as driving Building Alignment, 9*fig*; exchanging perspectives component for, 80, 81–84; know your audience questions to ask about, 101, 103; tips for, 88, 103; as two-way conversation, 80. *See also* Communication

Digital Equipment, 33

Doing the Work: Building Alignment guidelines for, 102–104; Championing Execution guidelines for, 149–151; Crafting the Vision guidelines for, 56–57. *See also* Work of Leaders program

Dragon spacecraft (SpaceX), 108

Drucker, Peter: contributions to thinking on leadership by, 4; on distinctions between management and leadership, 126; on taking risks, 33

Duffy, Gloria, 4

E

Edison, Thomas, 107, 110

8-Step Process for Leading Change, 115

Eliot, T. S., 23

Emerson, Ralph Waldo, 113
Emotional intelligence, 93
Everything DiSC 360 for Leaders (Inscape), 175
Exchanging perspectives: encouraging dialogue by, 80, 81–83; gaining buy-in by, 83; strategies for, 83–84
Execution: defined as making the vision a reality, 108–109; leadership commitment required for successful, 109. *See also* Championing Execution
Execution: The Discipline of Getting Things Done (Bossidy and Charan), 126–127
Exploration: boldness expanded to include, 174; comments from 360 survey on, 179t, 180t, 181t; as driving Crafting a Vision, 9fig; finding new opportunities through, 24–26; our built-in capacity for, 23–24; prioritizing the big picture for, 29–31; remaining open to new opportunities through, 26–29; tips for maximizing your, 31–32, 56
Exploring implications: strategies for, 49–50; testing assumptions by, 48–49

F
Fayol, Henri, 126, 127
Feedback: addressing problems type of, 137t, 138–142; asking people to provide their leaders with, 91; comments from 360 survey on, 179t, 180t, 181t; comments given to leaders about, 143t; comparing giving encouragement to giving positive, 94; as driving Championing Execution, 9fig, 135–146, 151; encouraging dialogue by asking for honest, 88; leaders' self-ratings on giving praise and addressing problems, 137t; offering praise type of, 137t, 142, 143t, 144–145; our favorite feedback outtakes, 189–192; as requiring active leader involvement, 136; tips for, 145–146; when learning a card game, 135–136. *See also* Quantitative and Qualitative Feedback
Feedback Outtakes, 189–192
The Fifth Discipline (Senge), 22, 79
First Principles of Instruction (Merrill), 184
The Five Dysfunctions of a Team (Lencioni), 86, 186
Franklin, Benjamin, 125
Frederick, Shane, 44
From Values to Action (Kraemer), 73

G
Galton, Sir Francis, 50
"Gaze of the audience," 84
George, Bill, 61
Gilbert, Daniel, 13
Girl Scouts, 15
Giving praise. *See* Offering praise
Goal-setting: crafting a Vision as driving, 20; momentum and establishment of, 115
Goals: BHAG ("Big Hairy Audacious Goal"), 20; initiating action to accomplish, 120–123; leaders who set high or low expectations and, 117–118t
Godin, Seth, 4, 64
Goleman, Daniel, 4, 93
Good to Great (Collins), 20
Gottman, John, 94
Group Facilitation vignette, 156–158

H
Harvard Business Review, 29
Harvard Business School, 107
Hesselbein, Frances, 4
High expectations, 117–118t
Holmes, Oliver Wendell, 69
Honeywell International, 127
Hoover Dam metaphor, 19–20

I

"I Have a Dream" (King speech), 14
Ideas: failure to test assumptions of your, 44–45; how vulnerability allows for sharing of, 87. *See also* Vision
IDEO, 39
In Search of Excellence (Peters), 114
Inclusiveness: shifted into Alignment with Clarity, 174; as vision-related leadership behavior, 165, 167t–173t
Individual Coaching vignette, 155–156
Infectious ambition, 117
Information: explaining rationale of, 72–75; monitoring for comprehension of, 74–75; need for accessible, 2–3; structuring message of, 75–76; training programs interest by type of, 2, 3t; transparency and access to essential, 74. *See also* Communication; Messages
Initiating action: creating momentum by, 120–122; redefining "above and beyond" for, 122; strategies for, 122–123
Innovation: as crucial element of boldness, 33–34; the Devil's Advocate as killer of, 40; fear of speaking out barrier to, 38–40
Innovative thinking skills training, 3t
The Innovator's Dilemma (Christensen), 33
Inscape's *Everything DiSC 360 for Leaders*, 175
Inspiration: aspects that leaders find most difficult, 164t; aspects that leaders find most difficult based on personality factors, 164t; being encouraging to provide, 94–96, 164t; being expressive to provide, 91–93, 164t; comments from 360 survey on, 179t, 180t; comparing how leaders rates themselves to how others do, 91; as driving Building Alignment, 9fig; gaining buy-in through, 90; know your audience questions to ask about what motivates them, 101, 103; self-ratings on adjectives associated with, 89–90t; tips for, 97, 104
International Mining Congress (Paris), 126
International Space Station, 108
iPhone, 108

J

Jobs, Steve, 15, 108

K

Kahneman, Daniel, 44, 45, 48–49, 186
Kampelman, Max M., 79
Kelleher, Herb, 14, 17
Keller, Helen, 13
Kelley, Tom, 39–40
Kellogg School of Management, 73
Kennedy, John F., 15
King, Martin Luther, Jr., 14
Klein, Gary, 49
Know your audience, 100–101, 102–103
Kotter, John, 115
Kouzes, Jim: *The Leadership challenge* co-authored by, 119; leadership perspective of, 4
Kraemer, Harry Jensen, Jr.: Change + Uncertainty = Chaos formula of, 73; on leader's hand-on role in execution, 127; leadership perspective of, 4

L

Labovitz, George, 99
Lacan, Jacques, 83–84
Langer, Ellen, 72
Lao-Tsu, 153
Law of Inertia, 114–115
Leader-follower relationship, 93
Leader surveys: comments about needing more clarity from leaders, 70–71t; difficulty of

remaining open versus seeking closure, 27t; experiences and sources that have most shaped leaders' development, 183t; finding new opportunities as most common request by employees, 24–25t; percentage of people making requests for improvement in their leaders, 176t–177t; percentage of those creating a strong vision, 18t–19; reasons given for not being bold, 34–35t; self-ratings on giving praise and addressing problems, 137t; of those who set high versus low expectations, 117–118t; what keeps you from speaking up about problems more often?, 139t. See also Analysis of 360-Degree Leadership Data; Teams

Leaders: comments made about feedback given by, 143t; experiences and sources that have most shaped development of, 183t; insecurity of inexperienced, 117; "Model the Way" behavior by, 119; optimistic, 95; "Six Critical Questions" for, 29–30, 31; tendency of so many to not seek counsel, 46–47; Work of Leaders as done by all levels of, 10

Leadership: creating a fresh set of assumptions about vision and, 16–17; different communication styles of, 71–72; including a broad range of perspectives on, 4; "The Myth of the Mountaintop" misconceptions about, 15–16; scholarship to understand the structure of, 165, 167t–173t; verifying and clarifying ideas on, 4–5. See also Management; Work of Leaders program

Leadership behaviors: Analysis of 360-Degree Leadership Data of, 6t, 162fig, 175–182; boldness, 165, 167t–173t; clarity, 165, 167t–173t; consultation, 165, 167t–173t; early factor analysis of vision-related, 165, 167t–173t; inclusiveness, 165, 167t–173t; multidimensional scaling analysis of, 165, 166fig; realism, 165, 167t–173t; risk management, 165, 167t–173t

The Leadership Challenge (Kouzes and Posner), 119

Leadership Literature Review: description of the, 6t; VAE development through scholarly review of, 161–163; Work of Leaders Development Pyramid position of, 162fig

Leadership Model Prototypes: description of, 6t; VAE development through study of, 182, 184; Work of Leaders Development Pyramid position of, 162fig

Leadership skills training, 2–3t

Lencioni, Patrick: *The Five Dysfunctions of a Team* by, 86, 186; leadership perspective of, 4; "Six Critical Questions" for leaders asked by, 29–30, 31

Levitt, Theodore, 29

Literature Review Update: description of, 7t; VAE model refinement using the, 186; Work of Leaders Development Pyramid position of, 162fig

Low expectations, 117–118t

Low, Juliette Gordon, 15, 17

Luthans, F., 74

M

Management: difference between leadership and, 125–126; Fayol's five functions of, 126, 127; interest in training to improve skills for, 3t. See also Leadership

Management theory, 126

"Marketing Myopia" (Levitt), 29

Matryoshka (Russian nesting toys), 22

Maxwell, John, 4, 114, 115

McGregor, Douglas, 63

"Mere exposure effect" experiment (1968), 76
Merrill, M. David, 184
Messages: achieving clarity by structuring, 75; sent by Type B personalities, 117; strategies for structuring, 75–76; "talking points" of, 76. *See also* Communication; Information
MIT, 63
"Model the Way" behavior, 119
Momentum: as always being toward the vision, 116; being driven component of, 116–120; comments from 360 survey on, 179*t*, 180*t*, 181*t*; creating a sense of urgency for, 115; as driving Championing Execution, 9*fig*, 113–123, 156; initiating action component of, 120–123; intuitive nature of, 114; leadership documentation on the power of, 114; Newton's first law on inertia and, 114–115; during organizational change, 115; tips for, 123
Motivation: being encouraging by tapping into their, 96; find out the audience, 101, 103
Multidimensional scaling analysis of leadership behaviors, 165, 166*fig*
"The Myth of the Mountaintop," 15–16

N

Need for closure (NFC): physical symptoms shown by people seeking, 27–28; remaining open versus, 27*fig*
Negativity, 95
New opportunities: exploration for finding new, 24–26; initiating action by jumping on, 120–123; as most common request for leaders, 24–25*t*; for offering praise, 145; remaining open to, 26–29

Newsweek magazine, 54
Newton's first law, 114–115
Noble causes strategy, 96
Nonverbal communication: being expressive through your, 93; verifying your receptiveness through your, 87, 88
Norman, S., 74

O

Offering praise: examples of, 143*t*; leaders' self-ratings on, 137*t*; providing feedback by, 142, 144; strategies for, 144–145
Ogilvy, David, 43
The One Thing You Need to Know (Buckingham), 95
Optimistic leaders, 95
Organizational change: Change + Uncertainty = Chaos formula for, 147; creating a sense of urgency for, 115; momentum during times of, 115; New opportunities for, 24–29, 120–123
Our Favorite Feedback Outtakes, 189–192
Ox weight estimate study (1907), 50

P

Pereira, William, 54
Personality Based Leadership Research: aspects of providing inspiration that are difficult based on personality factors, 164*t*; aspects of providing inspiration that are most difficult, 164*t*; description of the, 6*t*; Type A personality, 83; Type B personality, 117; VAE model development based on the, 163–165, 174; Work of Leaders Development Pyramid position of, 162*fig*
Peters, Tom: *In Search of Excellence* by, 114; singing the praises of momentum, 115
Pixar "criti" sessions, 138
"Political factors," 139*t*

Posner, Barry: *The Leadership Challenge* co-authored by, 119; leadership perspective of, 4
Praise. *See* Offering praise
"PreMortem" exercise, 49, 133
Primal Leadership (Goleman), 93
Prioritizing the big picture: finding new opportunities by, 29–30; strategies for, 30–31
The Program: as blueprint to execute the vision, 128; description and use of, 128–129
Progressive Architecture, 54
Projects: being aware of timing meetings on, 119–120; champions of, 109–110; explaining rationale for, 72–75; gaining buy-in for, 62, 83, 90; "prospective hindsight" facilitating success of, 49; providing a plan for, 128–131. *See also* Teams
"Prospective hindsight," 49
Providing a plan: executing structure by, 128–130; as iterative process, 130–131; strategies for, 130–131

Q
Quantitative and Qualitative Feedback: description of, 6t; VAE model refinement based on the, 185–186; Work of Leaders Development Pyramid position of, 162*fig*. *See also* Feedback
Questions: Championing Execution, 148–149; how alignment provides a forum for, 65–66; Lencioni's "Six Critical Questions" on what to ask, 29–30, 31; providing clarity by anticipating your audience, 101, 102; Supplemental Research follow-up alignment, 187t, 188t

R
Rationale: importance of explaining, 72–73; strategies for explaining, 73–75

Realism: merged into Testing Assumptions, 174; as vision-related leadership behavior, 165, 167t–173t
Remaining open: difficulty of NFC (need for closure) versus, 27t–28; finding new opportunities by, 26–28; strategies for, 28–29
Risk management: early factor analysis of, 167t–173t; as vision-related behavior, 165
Roets, Arne, 27

S
Sainte-Exupery, Antoine de, 89
Sears, 33
Seeking counsel: barriers to, 46–47; strategies for, 47–48; testing assumptions by, 46
Senge, Peter, 4, 22, 79
Sense of urgency, 115
Shaw, George Bernard, 135
Sims, Peter, 61
"Six Critical Questions" (Lencioni), 29–30, 31
Southwest Airlines, 14, 64
SpaceX, 108
Speaking out: boldness component of, 36, 38–40; how self-protective instincts influence our ability for, 39; "start" and "stop" time lapse in-class experiment, 38; strategies for, 40–41
Structure: analyzing in-depth to create, 131–133; comments from 360 survey on, 179t, 180t, 181t; as driving Championing Execution, 9*fig*, 125–134; 150–151; leadership role in providing, 125–126; providing a plan for, 128–131; tips for creating, 134
Structuring messages: achieving clarity by, 75; strategies for, 75–76; "talking points" of, 76
Stumbling on Happiness (Gilbert), 13
Subject-Matter Expert (SME) Reviews: description of, 6t; VAE

model development based on the, 184, 185; Work of Leaders Development Pyramid position of, 162*fig*

Succession Planning vignette, 158–160

The Super Moon Buffet restaurant, 1–2

Supplemental Research: alignment follow-up question 1 results, 187*t*; alignment follow-up question 2 results, 188*t*; description of, 7*t*; VAE model refinement using the, 187; Work of Leaders Development Pyramid position of, 162*fig*

Survey of Training Industry: description of, 6*t*; experiences and sources that have most shaped leaders' development, 183*t*; VAE model development based on the, 182; Work of Leaders Development Pyramid position of, 162*fig*

T

"Talking points" strategy: being expressive by using, 93; structuring messages for clarity by using, 76

Team meetings: being aware of timing for project, 119–120; exchanging perspectives during, 80, 81–84; Pixar "criti" sessions, 138

Team members: analyzing in-depth by, 131–133; differing needs of your, 129–130; gaining buy-in by the, 62, 83, 90; providing a plan to you, 128–131. *See also* Audience

Teams: analyzing in-depth process by, 131–133; commit to deadlines related to external events, 119; creating an environment with consistent and timely communication, 133; differing needs of small and large, 129–130; gaining buy-in by your, 62, 83, 90; how the Program keeps everyone on track, 128–129; initiating action as needed, 120–123; providing a plan to your, 128–131; traditional leader-follower relationship in, 93. *See also* Leader surveys; Projects

Technical knowledge training, 2, 3*t*

TED talks, 28

The Ten Faces of Innovation (Kelley), 39–40

Testing Assumptions: barriers to, 45–46; bat-and-ball puzzle as example of, 44; comments from 360 survey on, 181*t*; as driving Crafting a Vision, 9*fig*, 43–44; exploring implications for, 48–50; failure of actively, 44–45; seeking counsel for, 46–48; tips for, 50–51, 57

Theory X, 63

Theory Y, 63

Thinking Fast and Slow (Kahneman), 45

360-Degree Data. *See* Analysis of 360-Degree Leadership Data

Tips: for boldness, 41; for clarity, 77, 103; for dialogue, 88, 103; for exploration, 31–32; for feedback, 145–146; for inspiration, 97, 104; for momentum, 123; for structure, 134; for testing assumptions, 50–51

Trader Joe's, 64

Training magazine, 182

Training programs, 2, 3*t*

Transamerica Pyramid (San Francisco), 53–54

Transparency: when explaining rationale, 74; when learning a card game, 135–136

Tribal Leadership (Logan, King, and Fischer-Wright), 96

Tribes (Godin), 64

Trust: the process of crafting a vision, 55–56; vulnerability exercise for building, 86–87

Twain, Mark, 147
Type A personality, 83
Type B personality, 117

U
University of Michigan, 76
University of Minnesota, 38
"Use versus them" mentality, 95–96

V
VAE model: accuracy and accessibility priorities of the, 2–3, 8–9, 188; assumptions for vision within the, 16–17; Building Alignment component of, 5, 8, 9*fig*; Championing Execution component of, 5, 8, 9*fig*; Crafting a Vision component of, 5, 8, 9*fig*; ongoing alignment throughout the, 101–102; overview of the, 5, 8; results of building the, 188; ten stages of development in the, 5, 6*t*, 161–188*t*. *See also specific component*; Work of Leaders program
VAE model stages: 1: Leadership Literature Review, 6*t*, 161–163; 2: Personality Based Leadership Research, 6*t*, 162*fig*, 163–174; 3: Analysis of 360-Degree Leadership Data, 6*t*, 162*fig*, 175–182; 4: Survey of Training Industry, 6*t*, 162*fig*, 182; 5: Leadership Model Prototypes, 6*t*, 162*t*, 182–184; 6: Subject-Matter Expert (SME) Reviews, 6*t*, 162*fig*, 184; 7: Classroom Testing, 6*t*, 162*fig*, 185; 8: Quantitative and Qualitative Feedback, 7*t*, 162*fig*, 185–186; 9: Literature Review Update, 7*t*, 162*fig*, 186; 10: Supplemental Research, 7*t*, 162*fig*, 187*t*–188
VAE model vignettes: 1: Individual Coaching, 155–156; 2: Group Facilitation, 156–158; 3: Succession Planning, 158–160
van Hiel, Alain, 27

Vision: Building Alignment around a, 5, 8, 9*fig*, 62–67; choose the scope of the, 55; creating a fresh set of assumptions about leadership and, 16–17; as critical to a leader's work, 17; execution defined as making reality out of a, 108–109; Hoover Dam metaphor for a great, 19–20; how work is elevated by a truly great, 19; momentum as always being toward the, 116; "The Myth of the Mountaintop" misconceptions of, 15–16; the Program for executing the, 128–129; providing a plan to refine the, 128–131; ratings on percentage of leaders creating a strong, 18*t*–19; six different themes involved in creating a, 165, 167*t*–173*t*; three major benefits of an inspiring, 20; what we mean by, 14–17. *See also* Crafting a Vision; Ideas
Vision-related leadership behaviors: boldness as, 167*t*–173*t*; clarity as, 167*t*–173*t*; consultation as, 167*t*–173*t*; inclusiveness as, 167*t*–173*t*; leadership behavior of risk management used for, 167*t*–173*t*; realism as, 167*t*–173*t*; six different types of, 165, 174
Voice tone, 87, 88
Vulnerability exercise, 86–87

W
Wal-Mart, 108
Walton, Sam, 108
Wile E. Coyote (cartoon character), 131
Wiseman, Liz, 4
Wooden, John, 148–149
Work of Leaders Development Pyramid: Analysis of 360-Degree Leadership Data, 6*t*, 162*fig*, 175–182; Leadership Literature Review role in the, 6*t*, 161–163; Personality Based Leadership

Research role in the, 6t, 162fig, 163–165, 174
Work of Leaders program: cornerstone principles of the, 10; description of, 153–154; generating a personalized *Work of Leaders Profile,* 154; overview of the, 9fig; sample continua of, 154fig; vision as critical to, 17. *See also* Doing the Work; Leadership; VAE model
Work of Leaders vignettes: 1: Individual Coaching, 155–156; 2: Group Facilitation, 156–158; 3: Succession Planning, 158–160

X
Xerox, 33
Xerox line experiment, 72

Z
Zajonc, Robert: addressing patterns of leadership, 186; "mere exposure effect" experiments by, 76
Zeus, 15